PRAISE FOR ONE

"Tim's reputation speaks for itsel[illegible] thousands of people's lives around the world. Tim has been at rock bottom and climbed his way out. He definitely knows the formula for success. That's why I not only view him as a friend and colleague, but also as a mentor in helping me to impact even more lives on this planet. You, reader, have greatness within you! If you are looking to tap into and release your human potential, I highly recommend reading *One Belief Away!* by Tim Shurr. That's my story and I'm sticking to it!"

Les Brown—#1 Motivational Speaker in the World

"Timing is everything and now is the time for *One Belief Away!* at this tipping point in history. Tim, and his mentor, Joe, guide us step by step to a heightened awareness and offer specific actions we must take to overcome all the odds, invisible and real, to achieve authentic, lasting success. Tim Shurr is a change agent you can trust!"

Denis Waitley, Author of #1 All-Time Best-Selling Audio Program, *The Psychology of Winning*

"When evaluating a book, I look at the proportion of new and important information—versus padding and fluff. *One Belief Away!* is at the top of my list for providing the most useful, insightful, and beneficial information. Tim truly lives up to the excellence of this book!"

Mitzi Perdue (Mrs. Frank Perdue)—Author of *How to Make Your Family Business Last* and *How to Be UP in Down Times*

"Since over two million people have viewed my TEDx video, *How to Believe in Yourself,* I know there is a demand and a need for this book! Tim Shurr is a master at releasing people from limiting beliefs, and he should be your guide as well. I've studied with the masters in this field, and now I've discovered a new master, Tim Shurr. Truly, this book will help you make profound changes in your mind that will show up as breakthroughs in your life. I was inspired by Tim; you will be too."

Jim Cathcart, CSP, CPAE—Author of
The Acorn Principle* & *The Power Minute!

"There are plenty of great books that share deep wisdom about how to elevate your life. I've written many of them myself. However, Tim Shurr takes it a step farther by helping to reprogram your unconscious mind for greater love, faith, and prosperity! If you are looking for a book that will transform your life, you just found it!"

Chris Widener—Best Selling Author of *Lasting Impact*
and Hall of Fame Speaker

"This book is an invitation to explore the authentic side of who you are meant to be. Tim Shurr takes you on a sacred journey and will challenge you to come out of your comfort zone. *One Belief Away* is nourishment for your heart and soul. It is a book to be read again and again as a blessing in your life. If you are seeking a new way of seeing yourself, *One Belief Away* is the next step in your journey. Tim Shurr has been a blessing to me, and thousands of others. He will be this for you as well!"

Rev. Gretchen Schneider

One Belief Away is a gem. Of course I feel that way about it because I agree with all the wisdom and insights it presents to the reader. I have learned from my life as a surgeon caring for cancer patients and others, the power of the mind and beliefs. We create our future by our unconscious choices and our body believes what our mind conceives. I have seen what the mind can do and how hypnosis can induce incredible physical and emotional healing, which lead to the creation of an entirely new life for individuals who are willing to make changes. You can reparent yourself and turn a curse into a blessing. If you can love and believe in yourself, this book will be a valuable guidebook for you.

Bernie Siegel, MD author of *No Endings Only Beginnings* and *Love, Medicine & Miracles*

After over half a century of working in the field of personal growth, I'm totally convinced BELIEF is the stumbling block for the masses. This book will open a whole New World for you. *One Belief Away* can change your life forever. Tim Shurr and Joe Vitale are friends of mine. They are about to be your best friends!"

Bob Proctor, author of *You Were Born Rich* and *12 Power Principles For Success!*

"*One Belief Away* is a book that will capture you in the first few pages of reading it. It's THAT good. Not only does Tim transparently and genuinely share his own personal journey, but he provides us with the life-changing "road map" he used to break through. If you're tired of doing the work and getting nowhere, this book is the major "mindset reset" that you've been praying for! Thank you, Tim and Dr. Joe, for this wonderful, transformative gem!!"

Lisa Winston, #1 Best-Selling Author of *Your Turning Point,*" Co-host of the *Mindset Reset* TV Show

"In my book, *A Setback Is A Setup For A Comeback,* I shared a story about a man who went bankrupt and lost his house, his car, and his business. He was down and out. Then someone gave him materials to uplift him. He read the books and listened to the audios and the materials transformed his belief system. That man went on to turn his life around and become a multi-millionaire. One new belief can transform your life and your legacy! Tim Shurr and Dr. Joe Vitale have written a book entitled *One Belief Away,* and it is a book that will help you change your life and your legacy! Read it and then re-read it, and get ready for the rest of your life to become the best of your life!"

Dr. Willie Jolley, Hall of Fame Speaker and Best selling author of *It Only Takes A Minute To Change Your Life!*

One Belief Away!

How to Upgrade Your Unconscious Mind for Prosperity and Inner Peace!

Tim Shurr, MA
and
Dr. Joe Vitale

Published by Shurr Success, Inc.

For general information on our other products and services, please visit TimShurr.com or call 877-944-HOPE.

Library of Congress Cataloging-in-Publication Data:
Shurr, Tim, 1970
Vitale, Joe, 1953
one belief away:

ISBN 0-9670408-9-2
Hardcover ISBN 978-1-64184-426-0
1. Success.

Printed in the United States of America
10 9 8 7 6 5 4 3 2 1

TABLE OF CONTENTS

Good job investing in yourself!

As a reward, Dr. Joe and Tim wish to share a few bonus resources that will help speed up your growth and results while going through the One Belief Away experiences in the book.

Head over to www.survivingtothriving.me/obabonus and claim the following tools:

- **The Power Of Your Unconscious Mind** By Tim Shurr, MA This 5-video and audio training course reveal the secrets of how to unleash the full power of your mind!
- A Simple Way to Eliminate Doubts & Excuses Guidebook by Dr. Joe Vitale.
- 2 Special Video Conversations between Dr. Joe and Tim that helped form the content of this book.

Enjoy using the power of your mind to create your life by design!

As Dr. Joe says, "Onwards and upwards!"

FOREWORD

I met Tim Shurr about twenty years ago. We connected and stayed in touch. When he said he had an idea for a book we could create together, I not only listened but also quickly agreed. After an entire year of back and forth discussions, emails, audio messages, and drafts, I'm pleased to announce that this is the long-awaited book. We are both excited to bring it to you, and here's why.

Tim and I wanted to help people who felt like they weren't being helped by other books or tools. Far too many people think, "That stuff works for others, but not for me." We wanted to help those people. We want to help *you*.

We also wanted to satisfy the critics, who can find fault with rainbows. We considered their most hardened arguments and did our best to address them. Anybody who reads this book and still feels the material is nonsense simply doesn't *want* to be helped. Period.

With these audiences in mind, we went deep in creating a short, easy, but deep book on how to *really* create the life you want—in spite of your background, your story, your perceived limitations, or much else.

The material in this book works! Others just like you have tested it in the frontlines of life, and both Tim and I have also put it to the test for decades. We have lived and still live this stuff. We teach it because it gets results.

If you are ready for results too, then turn the page and—as I like to say—*Expect Miracles!*

Love,
Dr. Joe Vitale
www.MrFire.com

ACKNOWLEDGMENTS

I'd like to tell you my original aspirations were to solve life's mysteries and bring more inner peace into the world. But that is false. My life has been dedicated to eliminating my personal struggles with anxiety, insecurity, and the need for others' approval. Through the years, I've experienced hundreds of heartbreaks and letdowns, and if there was a mistake to be made, I seemed to be first in line to make it.

Through the constant search to alleviate my fears, I'd stumble upon a new idea, technique, or philosophy and feel comfortable, only to fall back into old habits and patterns time and again. I didn't know why this kept happening and often felt like things were never going to work out the way I wanted them to. My only saving grace was the commitment to keep moving forward no matter what. Now that might seem inspiring, but honestly, it didn't stem from being courageous. Instead, it came from not knowing what else to do but take another step in a direction that offered hope.

The most considerable breakthroughs occurred by becoming a hypnosis coach and facilitating thousands of sessions where clients shared their deepest, darkest fears with me. Through those stories of abuse, trauma, shame, guilt, and anger, I began noticing that although the details of the experiences varied, the unconscious beliefs shared by so many people were exactly the same. Here is the programming billions of people are unconsciously walking around with.

> "I'm not good enough and unworthy or deserving of love (or success). Since I don't feel loved, protected, or encouraged, there is something inherently wrong with me. As a result, I cannot fully love and accept myself or create a life of fulfillment."

This is the root of all anxiety and human suffering. If you are alive, you will experience physical and emotional pain. It's unavoidable. However, much of our human *suffering* is optional, and often, unconsciously self-inflicted. Most are unaware that your beliefs, and not your circumstances, are what are causing your despair or failed attempts at attaining desirable goals. I began applying a combination of therapeutic techniques to upgrade this unconscious programming for clients, and what happened next felt like a miracle!

I unearthed a set of transformational exercises that consistently freed people from the traumas and limiting beliefs of their past. It worked every time, regardless of what they came in for. I started getting a reputation for being a miracle worker, which couldn't be further from the truth. I simply learned how to help people authentically love and accept themselves while upgrading their beliefs about what's possible. This newfound security and freedom allowed them to achieve goals that once felt impossible to attain. It can do the same for you!

If you picked this book up because you're looking to achieve goals or make more money, the strategies inside would help you do that. After all, you're often only one belief away from living life on your terms! This journey is also for those like me who struggle with anxiety and insecurity because of a turbulent past. If you've been hurt, I'll show you how to quickly put the tiny pieces of your heart back together again! The journey you're about to take is graceful and empowering. The speed at which you'll attain significant results will impress you.

I'm still working on being the best me that I can be. I'm not perfect by a long shot, but that's okay because, flaws and all,

I love and accept myself. I'm no longer ruled by shame, guilt, or feeling small. I get insecure and anxious occasionally, but I embrace those feelings with curiosity rather than dread. This has created a state of joy and fulfillment that's unlocked a sea of opportunities and blessings. Yet, I still have much to learn, so I convinced an authority on personal development to help fill in the blanks wherever I needed help. I will be forever grateful that my friend, Dr. Joe Vitale, said yes and agreed to help with this book's creation. Together, we will help you discover how mesmerizing you actually are!

I'd also like to thank my wife, Stacey, for her unconditional love and encouragement. She's sacrificed so much to support my career. Her wisdom and high moral standards have made the most substantial impact on my life. I would not be who I am today without her kindness, guidance, and unbelievable patience!

I've also learned a tremendous amount about the power of love and courage from my two extraordinary boys, Maximus and Aiden. Each day, they help me become more patient, generous, and thoughtful. Ultimately, they drive me to show up each day at my best so I can be as much of an example for them, as they are for me.

I also want to thank Pastor Gretchen Schneider for her proofreading skills and continuous encouragement and Randy Gage for telling me the original title for this book was horrible. He was right! It's a blessing to have friends who will tell you the truth, even if it stings.

Also, a huge thank you to Chris O'Byrne and his incredible team at JetLaunch.net. Teri Kojetin made the publishing process seamless and Debbie O'Byrne designed the magical cover of this book. They are brilliant!

I'd like to also thank all my clients I've had the sincere privilege of serving over the years. Through the pain and turmoil came the victories and triumphs!

Finally, I want to thank *you*, dear reader. If you were drawn to this book, we share more in common than you may realize, and it's an honor to join you on this awe-inspiring journey! As my dear friend Les Brown says, "You have greatness within you!" It's time to unleash it!

Love & Laughter,
Tim Shurr, MA

PREFACE

If you don't want to go without, look within!

Do you have a goal or dream you're struggling to achieve? Or perhaps you desire a sense of inner peace, rather than wrestling with anxiety most of the day. Have you tried to overcome traumas from your past, but they just won't let you move on? If you find yourself in one of these three situations—and almost everyone will at one time or another—the answers and solutions you seek are in this book.

Ever wonder what's holding you back, or why you haven't attained it yet? In almost every case, it's because of the self-sabotaging beliefs running like malware (software virus) in your brain. The unconscious opinions you've formed about yourself, others, your situation, or the world around you determine whether you will succeed at turning your goals into a reality or not.

It may seem obvious then to identify and change beliefs if they keep you stuck. Yet, unconscious attitudes are the last things most seek to improve. Instead, we blame others or attempt to change our environment, and that's why so many never find the breakthroughs they seek. Today, this vicious cycle of disappointment ends for you!

Perhaps you've tried applying willpower to get what you want. If so, you realize willpower lasts about two minutes before fizzling away, and then your emotional programming takes over. It's like when the older versions of my smartphone would flash *10% battery life* and then immediately shut down. Logic and common sense have much less to do with people's behavior than most realize. Whenever someone with Type 2 diabetes grabs a soda, or a smoker lights up a cigarette, they know that logically it's a bad idea. Yet, their emotional programming causes them to engage in those unhealthy behaviors anyway.

A veteran who served in the Vietnam War once came to see me for PTSD. He said, "The other day, I was standing in the middle of a department store and suddenly heard the whooshing sound of a Huey helicopter as it flew over the store. Without thinking, I hit the ground. I had an intense feeling of anxiety wash over me, and it felt like I couldn't control my body. In the service, certain sounds meant trouble, and the Huey helicopter makes a very recognizable noise as the twin blades cut through the air. Even though I rationally knew I was safe in that store, I emotionally reacted out of pure instinct because of experiences from my past. What's worse is the embarrassment I felt when seeing the shocked expressions from the other shoppers." (I helped him eliminate those traumatic responses using the tools in this book.)

Emotions regularly overrule logic and common sense. Thus, you will learn how to reprogram your emotional mind to enhance the way you feel and behave each day. From thirty years of helping people achieve their goals, I've discovered the precise beliefs and thought patterns that lead to inner peace and prosperity. I've also learned how to eliminate the harmful head trash that holds us back from reaching our full potential.

Maybe you are a strong, Type A personality and have applied sheer force to cause things to work out for you in life. But the *big* goals you desire still seem out of reach, even with all your hard work and effort. Or, maybe you've learned to channel your anxiety into achieving big goals, and now you're tired of being stressed and discontent even after reaching them. Again, these are signals that the self-limiting beliefs embedded in your unconscious mind need upgrading. Nobody wants to hear that, especially if you've been working on personal development for years. Yet, it still holds, which is why I wrote this book and reached out to one of the world's foremost experts on the manifesting of goals and prosperity, Dr. Joe Vitale. His powerful methods for manifesting abundance, combined with my proven strategies for quickly upgrading unconscious programming, provide a clear path for increasing health, wealth, and peace of mind.

My passion for helping others eliminate needless emotional suffering was rooted in the desire to end my own. The journey for me began in 1982 when I was twelve years old. I remember sitting in my kitchen in Hobart, Indiana, when the telephone rang. After I answered it, the woman on the other end said urgently, "Honey, get your mom. There's been an accident!" My dad was an electrician at a steel mill. While working on a large electrical panel, somebody turned it on, which caused an explosion. The fire left my father with third-degree burns from the waist up, and we weren't sure he would live through it.

I didn't see my dad again for a couple of months as he fought for his life in the Loyola Burn Center in Illinois. The first time I visited him in the burn unit, they brought him out in a wheelchair, wrapped like a mummy in gauze. Walking through a burn unit when you're a kid and hearing people screaming is horrible enough. But then to see your dad like that was terrifying! I won't go into the gory details because we all have our war stories from childhood. The good news is my dad got through it and eventually came home. Even though he underwent several skin graft surgeries, he was still the first guy to take off his shirt and swim in the summertime. His scars were on the outside, yet mine lay hidden on the inside.

I stopped playing life to win and started playing *not to lose.* Do you know what happens when you play not to lose? You feel like you're always losing, even when you're not. I spent the first half of my life waiting for the next bad thing to happen. Often, bad things did happen because whatever you look for enough, you find. These hurtful experiences reinforced my fearful beliefs. The coping strategies I developed to deal with the anxiety only made things worse. I was in a destructive cycle and had no idea how to get out of it.

It wasn't until my senior year in high school that I had my first glimpse of hope. I took an introductory psychology class and learned about the "father of modern psychology," Dr. William James. He said, "The greatest discovery of the 20th century is that your thinking determines the quality of your life." In other words, **you can change your life by improving your thoughts!** I decided to enter the field of clinical psychology so I could learn how to get my mind to prepare me rather than scare me. After several years and completing thirty-one psychology courses in college and graduate school, I realized traditional forms of talk therapy were antiquated. People were spending their whole lives undergoing psychotherapy and never experiencing significant breakthroughs. Yuck! I didn't want to spend my entire life repeatedly telling the same sob stories to a therapist. I wanted practical solutions to help me change how I was feeling now.

Luckily, something beautiful and unexpected happened while sitting in a psychological interventions course during my sophomore year of college. A clinical hypnotherapist came in as a guest lecturer. He explained that the mind was mighty. You could use it to accomplish extraordinary results, often much faster than through talk therapy alone. He told how one could program the unconscious mind rather than relying solely on conscious willpower and positive thinking. He then asked for a volunteer to demonstrate how quickly someone could access a deep state of physical relaxation. I knew nothing about hypnosis, and I thought it would be fun to cluck like a chicken, so I volunteered.

That's when the miracle occurred! The hypnotist asked me to pay attention to my breathing. He guided me through a series of mental activities, like walking down a flight of stairs in my mind. I remember feeling so peaceful and at ease. I knew what was going on around me, and I could hear some of the other students laughing, yet I didn't care. At that moment, I realized the anxious knot I had always carried around in my stomach had disappeared. I felt nothing but peace. The hypnotist then said I'd feel more confident in the week ahead and had me open my eyes.

The next week, I felt more confident. I couldn't explain why; I just did. Eventually, the knot in my stomach reappeared because I was good at making myself feel anxious. Although, at the time, I didn't realize my beliefs were causing the anxiety. However, the realization lingered that my mind could create feelings of peace very quickly. From that moment, I began looking into schools that taught clinical hypnotism, which is used therapeutically and not for entertainment. I found a hypnotism school a couple of hours away and begged the instructor to enroll me. Her students consisted of medical doctors and dentists; I was a second-year psychology student. Yet, she allowed me to attend, and it transformed the course of my life forever.

Receiving education on hypnotism opened doors to all kinds of peak performance technologies taught outside of traditional psychology training. I was both amazed and skeptical about the anecdotal success stories and miracles people were experiencing. I had a "prove it" mentality and didn't believe miracle breakthroughs were happening just because somebody said they were. I wanted to see it for myself. I began taking classes and courses in a wide variety of holistic modalities like Healing Touch, Reiki, tai chi, qigong, and meditation. Then I was introduced by Dr. John Harris, professor of Psychology at Valparaiso University, to NLP (Neuro-Linguistic Programming).

NLP is the study of the psychological strategies that lead to high achievement. It's the mind's roadmap and helps unveil the subconscious recipes and formulas that generate success or failure, happiness, or depression. Over the years, I've also studied EMDR (Eye Movement Desensitization and Reprocessing), kinesiology, and EFT (Emotional Freedom Techniques). I've been testing the effectiveness of these interventions for over thirty years with tens of thousands of clients. Out of all the tools acquired, the insights and techniques from hypnotism and NLP have consistently produced the most astounding, consistent, and reliable results for clients, regardless of the presenting problem or issue.

A dear friend and former student, Roger Harris, recently posted, "What is extraordinary to us is just another day at Tim's office." The real credit goes to the pioneers of these peak performance fields who've created life-changing tools that most don't even know exist. I've embedded numerous insights, success formulas, and techniques into this book. Through reading the following chapters, you will gain wisdom and power over your destiny that few have ever experienced/

The information and mental reprogramming exercises in the journey ahead will enable you to make proactive, life-enhancing breakthroughs in ways you might not believe possible. You'll uncover the beliefs, emotions, and habits that are sabotaging your efforts and overcome them. Whatever feels unattainable will now become within reach. Today begins a new chapter in your life, and it's going to be a good one!

THE JOURNEY AHEAD

The first leg of your journey from surviving to thriving is devoted to cultivating a confident and resilient mindset because it's the foundation of all success. If you don't have a prosperous attitude, the best-made plans for achieving peace and prosperity won't matter. Self-limiting beliefs will keep you from consistently following through on your goals or putting effort in the right areas. You are going to develop a world-class mindset and gain secrets for having sustainable focus and motivation. Imagine what you'll be able to do with this!

You will also learn how to program your unconscious mind, the part controlling 80% of your decisions and behaviors, to follow through on actions that lead to the results you desire. Many say they know what to do but cannot get themselves to take action consistently. That happens because fearful beliefs and ineffective motivational strategies are at play. There's no getting around doing the inner work if you wish to see better results in life. You can recite positive affirmations and create stunning vision boards all day long. Yet, if you don't upgrade the limiting beliefs responsible for your frustrations, those techniques won't produce sustainable results. You've got to dive into your unconscious mind and update your core beliefs to create lasting breakthroughs.

Because most don't know how to upgrade their unconscious programming, they attempt to improve their lives through improving external situations, rather than doing the inner work. Bariatric weight loss surgeries are an extreme example of this. Some people feel they cannot stop eating any other way except through surgically modifying their internal organs. Instead of addressing the emotional issues that lead to obesity or compulsive eating, the goal is to alter the body (external) rather than upgrade the mindset (internal). This invasive surgery can give some of the boosts they need. The latest research suggests 70% of bariatric patients regain all the lost weight within a year of having the surgery. It's what happens when you attempt to modify external factors (change your physical body) without editing your internal programming (addressing weight loss's emotional aspect). If you don't upgrade self-limiting beliefs and remove emotional eating triggers, you'll fall back into the same eating habits that initially led to becoming obese.

The second leg in this journey is devoted to helping you gain greater clarity about how you want your life to be. Most consume themselves with what they are unhappy with or what they do not possess. I once asked a new client what she wanted to accomplish during our coaching sessions.

She said, "I want to stop procrastinating."

I replied, "That's what you're attempting to get away from, but what do you want?"

Puzzled, she said, "I just want to stop putting things off."

One of her challenges was that she hadn't provided a clear message to her subconscious mind about what to accomplish. Instead, she focused on the obstacles in the way, and hence, found more of them. Your brain moves you in the direction that you concentrate on most. The more she thought about "not procrastinating," the more she put things off because her attention was on "not" doing something. Imagine jumping into a cab, and the driver asks, "Where do you want to go?" You reply, "Well, I don't want to go to the bank, grocery store, or pub." That answer doesn't explain where you want to end up, so most stay put. As Dr. Phil once said, "You got to name it, to claim it."

In your journey's final leg, you'll go through enlightening "prosperity experiences" for upgrading beliefs, self-confidence, prosperity, and inner peace. These experiences are what separates this book from other self-help books on the market. I won't provide you with lofty ideas for *what* to do to create a fulfilling life and then expect you to do it. That's how you find yourself in the same place you started in before reading a book. Instead, I'll show you *how* to get yourself to follow through and make impactful upgrades in your life. We will dive deep into your unconscious mind, unearth and release hurts and blocks from the past, and install an "abundance consciousness" within you.

You will be mentally and emotionally reprogrammed to think, feel, and behave in a more empowered way for the rest of your life. Willpower does not last. Intentionally developed and reinforced habits do. The goal is for you to experience an internal shift in the way you understand the world around you, and we are going to do this together, step by step.

Sometimes, people fear that the emotional transformation they desire will take a long time and require a tremendous amount of effort, struggle, or pain to accomplish. These are false ideas that were born from people going through counseling programs and never getting better. In my three decades of practice, I've found the opposite to be true. My clients make breakthroughs lightning fast, they enjoy the process, and the results are sustainable.

It requires the same amount of energy, time, and effort to support or sabotage your efforts. As you assimilate these teachings into your life, you'll spend a lot more time having fun, producing results, and less time stewing in worry. When first beginning their new journey, clients will often say, "I hope this works." My reply is always, "You don't need to hope. That's what you've hired me for, and we *will* succeed!" They usually smile because they want someone with that level of confidence leading them. Occasionally, they will ask, "How are you so confident?" I reply, "Because I've watched people go from breakdowns to breakthroughs right in front of me so many thousands of times that I know this process works, and soon, you will too!"

Magic, Waiting to Be Released!

Annually, I host a profoundly life-enhancing two-day retreat entitled, *Design Your Destiny*. People from around the world attend to personally take them through the "Prosperity Experiences" that you will soon be going through in this book. During one of the retreats, Wendy, a woman in her mid-fifties, attended. Her big goal was to conquer the claustrophobia that had her practically homebound. She had struggled with this since the age of eight, and it had dramatically held her back. Wendy was afraid to get into elevators, ride in cars, drive herself, fly in airplanes, or be in closed spaces. It was amazing she was able to muster the courage to attend my event. If it weren't for her incredibly supportive children, sister, and nieces bringing her in and picking her up each day, she wouldn't have come.

During the event, Wendy began to look at herself and her capabilities in a more empowered way. We identified where her fears came from, upgraded the belief that drove her claustrophobia, and equipped her with a series of strategies for feeling "in charge" regardless of her environment. After the retreat ended, Wendy pulled me aside and pointed at an elevator. "I want to go in there," she said. I knew the moment of truth had arrived.

I accompanied Wendy into the elevator while gently reminding her of what to do once inside. As soon as the doors closed, Wendy grabbed my arm and started breathing heavily. I immediately instructed her to use the tools we had practiced, and I joined her in using them. As she began using her Power Breathing and firing the Confidence Anchor, her anxiety began decreasing. We climbed up to the ten-story building. By the time we descended back down to ground level, Wendy's anxiety transformed from fear to utter joy. She had conquered her greatest fear! Yet, that wasn't even the best part. What happened next was even more spectacular.

Wendy's family had come to pick her up, and they quietly observed Wendy and I enter the elevator. They told us later they were shocked to see this and had anxiously gathered in front of the elevator door, ready to comfort her. Instead, when the elevator doors opened, they saw Wendy spontaneously throw her arms in the air in a sign of victory! Her family cheered, and Wendy ran toward them as a steady flow of tears, hugs, and cheers filled the hallway. It still chokes me up every time I tell this story.

Wendy had struggled with claustrophobia for forty-five years, and it severely held her back. Imagine the amount of time and energy she unwittingly wasted on worrying. Yet, her newfound confidence sparked a wave of transformations, including her ability to board a plane and visit her son halfway across the country. I tell you this story because what Wendy was able to accomplish, you can as well. Regardless of your challenges, you can rise above them and excel. It doesn't have to take ten years or even one year to accomplish these breakthroughs. You will start getting results almost immediately as you go through the experiences along this journey.

How to Proceed

I have numerous stories of how people overcame lifelong mental blocks and triumphed over obstacles they once thought were insurmountable. You're going to receive the same tools and mind-conditioning exercises these clients used to better their lives so that you can improve yours. The following are three guidelines to help make this happen smoothly.

1. Have fun with this experience! People learn faster when they are enjoying themselves.

2. Keep an open mind. These tools and insights have benefitted thousands of people. As silly as some may seem (I do that on purpose), they produce extraordinary results.

Do the work first, and then analyze the results. Doing the opposite is self-sabotage.

3. Follow the instructions I've laid out and put as much into each "Prosperity Experience" as possible. The more you invest in this, the more you'll get out of it.

Since this book takes you on a journey, I recommend working through one chapter per day. Each one contains a lesson and experiential exercise that builds you up for the next step along the path. You may spread the journey out or work diligently through the chapters. Either way is okay. Just don't rush through the book. The point isn't to get the book read, but to enjoy what you'll discover about yourself.

Warning: A few of these transformation exercises may make you feel uncomfortable. One of the big secrets for cultivating inner peace and abundant prosperity is to learn how to *be comfortable being uncomfortable!* It's only outside your comfort zone that you'll find your most substantial breakthroughs. You can't play it safe and grow at the same time. Be courageous, which means feel the fear and do it anyway. As philosopher Lao Tse once said, "You must go out on a limb because that's where the fruit is."

Do the exercises half-heartedly, and you will get mediocre results. Follow through and trust that each "test" you pass along the path sets you up to succeed down the road, and your results will be stellar. Keep reading if you're ready for a brand-new approach with powerful tools that will get you:

1. Believing in you.
2. Following through on actions that lead to *you* getting what you want.
3. Developing successful habits that continually attract joy and prosperity into your life.

It's time for you to experience the pleasure, freedom, and security of feeling empowered. Sit up straight with high energy.

Push your shoulders back, lift your chin, and take three deep breaths through your nose, down to your belly. Then say out loud, **"My mind and heart are now open to receiving abundant wisdom, peace, and prosperity!"**

You are now ready.

It's time for your journey of a lifetime to begin!

"You must go out on a limb because that's where the fruit is!"

Lao Tse

CHAPTER 1
YOUR JOURNEY BEGINS

"Obstacles are what you see when you take your eyes off your goals."

Brian Tracy

LAYING THE FOUNDATION FOR INNER PEACE AND PROSPERITY

You have a goal, a dream. The first mental shift you must make is to decide you will succeed in turning your dreams into a reality. It is in this decisive moment that you become halfway there. **Self-belief is the only element that separates those who win from those who don't.** Self-belief allows you to continue striving for what you want when others have long given up or think you're crazy.

Whether useful or self-sabotaging, your beliefs determine the kind of life you experience, which is why it's essential to uncover unconscious beliefs that hold you back and then upgrade them before doing anything else. It's always the first step in cultivating inner peace and abundant prosperity. If you don't replace beliefs that hold you back with ones that move you forward, all the world's positive thinking won't do much good.

If you are going to upgrade your beliefs, let's clarify what they are first. Do you think a belief is a fact or an opinion? They are opinions you perceive with certainty to be true. They are subjective interpretations of how you experience others, the world around you, and yourself. What's the difference between a belief and a fact? In English, we call a dog, dog. Regardless of the type of species, it's still a dog. That's a fact. Whether you like dogs or believe them to be enjoyable pets is an opinion. At one time, worldly scholars once thought the world was flat, and all the planets revolved around Earth. Even though this was an accepted theory, and punitive for not agreeing, this opinion was still false. The reality is the world is slightly oblong, and our planet revolves around the sun. Facts are always accurate, whether one agrees with them or not. Beliefs, however, are viewpoints that you can decide to accept, reinforce, or change (upgrade).

Are you a person worthy of love, respect, and prosperity? Who decides this? Many believe those who raised them determine one's level of self-worth. But that would only be the opinion of their caregiver. There's only one individual in charge of selecting your deservedness of love, respect, and prosperity. It's *you!*

How Beliefs Are Formed

Beliefs are opinions you feel are correct or accurate. They typically form in three ways: through heightened emotional experiences, repetition, or misinterpretation. Let's go through each one.

I used to have a fear of public speaking. The belief was, "I can't (comfortably) speak in front of groups." Since I wasn't born with this perspective, how did I end up with it? The first way was through a series of heightened emotional experiences that negatively impacted me at a subconscious level. Whenever I got called upon to talk in front of the class, it activated my fight-or-flight response in grade school. My heart would pound, my throat got dry, and my hands would shake. As a result of this, my brain formed the opinion that "I can't speak in public" as a defense mechanism to protect me from the fearful feelings and perceived threat of humiliation. "If I can't speak in front of groups, I can use it as a shield to protect me from feeling anxious." Your brain has been developing unconscious (out of your conscious awareness) survival strategies since you were born. Unfortunately, some of these approaches create more problems than they prevent.

Beliefs can also instantly form when an authority figure (parent, teacher, preacher) says something to you while you are feeling highly emotional. Many who fear public speaking have recounted how teachers, or nuns in their Catholic school, would make sarcastic remarks or say demoralizing things to them as they stood in front of the class. The public ridicules for not knowing the answers, or freezing up, instantly internalized a belief in them that "I'm not smart" or "I can't speak in front of groups."

The second way beliefs form is through repetition. I had to give several presentations all through high school. From the moment I found out I had to provide a presentation in front of the class, I began telling myself, "I can't do this" and visualized passing out, freezing up, and being utterly humiliated. By the time it was my turn to present, I was so riddled with worry, I could barely get through it, which only strengthened the belief. I'd also see other students having near panic attacks while showing their work in front of the class, which further fueled my fear.

Because of the intensity of my emotional reaction, the idea that I could not speak comfortably in front of others was a fact in my mind, not an opinion. Yet, over the years, I've provided hundreds of public programs speaking to tens of thousands of people—and I loved it! So which belief is true? Am I afraid of public speaking, or do I love it? Even though my original fear of public speaking felt like a fact, it was only a belief, and beliefs can change.

The third way beliefs form is through misinterpretation. Most psychologists agree that most viewpoints that guide your adult decisions are in place by the age of twelve. Imagine an inner twelve-year-old in charge of your health, money, and relationships. That might sound silly, yet watch how adults behave when stressed. Some of us had extremely immature parents who, intentionally or not, said or did things that caused us to believe we were inadequate, unworthy, or not enough. Yet, this is the misinterpretation of a child because, at that age, most do not have the conscious awareness or wisdom to realize that it's your parent who has the issue, not you.

As a father, I've had to do a lot of maturing. I grew up in the 1970s, and everyone I knew was sarcastic. We were always ripping on each other. Parents teased their kids, and we all kidded each other. It was supposed to be playful, but most didn't realize how detrimental words could be. Because my anxiety and insecurities were sky-high, I used humor to defuse situations and gain approval from peers. Regrettably, as a result, I said and did a lot of rude things just to get a laugh. When I became a dad, my wife informed me that this behavior would not be acceptable. I felt offended at the time, but it was sage advice.

As a result, my kids experienced very little sarcasm until they began attending school. I rarely teased or mocked them. Yet, occasionally, I'd make a silly remark, not realizing my oldest son would take it seriously. Without hesitation, my wife would immediately point it out to me, and I'd feel terrible. Then, I'd sit my son down, apologize, explain what I should have said, and then fill his head with supportive, loving words and affirmations. To this day, I appreciate my wife for the two amazing teenagers we have. But not everyone is lucky enough to have an enlightened parent. In that situation, we must "re-parent" ourselves by cleaning up the misinterpretations of our childhood.

I remember the incident that turned around my opinion about public speaking. During my senior year of high school, the teacher of my interpersonal relationships class informed us the final exam would be a class presentation. We got to choose our topic, and I wasn't sure what to do. As if on cue, my nerves kicked in. But then, a moment of inspiration struck! What if I gave a speech on the fear of public speaking? I could freak out like normal, but make it look like it was part of the presentation.

I wrote down all the symptoms I felt when giving a public lecture and then pointed them out during the actual presentation.

I talked about how my hands would shake and then shook them vigorously while holding my notes. I spoke of my knees knocking together, my mouth getting dry, and my heart pounding as I mimed these actions like a game of charades. Everyone was laughing, and some kids fell out of their chairs! Even the teacher was giggling in the back of the classroom. I started laughing myself and became more relaxed. When the talk concluded with my saying, "the end" and taking a bow, the class erupted in applause. I felt terrific, and then it happened. My teacher yelled out from the back of the room, "That was the best presentation I ever heard! I wish we would have recorded it!" Since I was highly emotional, this new opinion soared into my brain and became my new truth. "I enjoy public speaking, and I'm good at it!"

I've been reinforcing those two beliefs ever since. I'll be fifty years old when this book is published. A few months ago, I provided a keynote at the Society of Human Resources convention. I received sixty-five five-star ratings from attendees, and many of the written comments said, "Best presentation I have ever seen!" I wish I could remember the teacher's name from my high school interpersonal communications class so I could thank her.

What Thoughts Are You Reinforcing?

Whatever you hear or say enough will become your destiny. Even opinions or ideas you don't believe at first can become absorbed as truth if you listen to them enough. For instance, if your father said out of anger that you would never amount to anything, you may not believe him. Even though it hurts your feelings, you'd recognize that he was just mad. However, if he regularly commented, odds are you'd start believing him and acting accordingly.

Cognitive researchers suggest that, on average, people are subject to approximately 180,000 critical or derogatory remarks by the time they are eighteen years old. (If you grew up in the 1970s, it might be double that!) That translates into about 25,000 hours of negativity pumped into your brain during your most crucial time of development. Research has also found that 80%

of this negative programming occurs before you're ten years old, which is when your foundational beliefs about others, the world, and yourself also form. In the new world of social media, these numbers may still be increasing.

People have had so much negativity pounded into their brains as kids that it's no surprise that it continues to plague us as adults. Many of my clients have said, "It's like I have this negative record playing over and over in my head, telling me how worthless I am." As a child, you didn't have the mental awareness to understand all the circumstances driving the comments others made to you. What if your dad was having a horrible day and said, "You're the reason for all my money problems!" You probably wouldn't have the mental maturity at seven years old to say, "Actually, Father, you are responsible for your issues with money, and you're taking them out on me. I'm sure you are just having a bad day and blowing off steam. I know you love me and will probably feel bad about your comment later. I'm going to go play." Imagine if we could all have a mental filter like that in place! Perhaps we can.

Instead of filtering out why people make derogatory comments, one's mental filter gets clogged with self-doubt. The father's comment about you being the reason for his money problems would instead be interpreted to mean that you are a burden on the family. Some take it even further, thinking they shouldn't have been born at all. It's such a common misconception that there's a term for it. According to Dr. William Barnett, in his outstanding book, *Unlock Your Mind and Be Free*, he refers to this as the Crime of Existence. He suggests it's like having a trial jury in your unconscious mind and being found guilty without having all the evidence. Your sentence is confinement to the limitations of your negative beliefs. Each self-sabotaging fear is a bar that makes up your mental prison. Your goal is to have a new trial as an adult, introduce evidence that proves your innocence, and immediately free yourself.

As kids, we don't have much power or control over what happens to us. However, as adults, we do. You can take on a whole new perspective that shifts the old beliefs you used to carry around inside your mind. For example, perhaps you are now a parent. Have you ever had a bad day or let stress get the best of you, and then you said something to your kid you wish you could take back? I certainly have. It's in those moments where we realize how our parents might have been feeling, and it wasn't as personal as we took it in our youth.

Allow me to share an example from a client of mine. Ray had always felt disconnected from his father after his parents' divorce. When I asked about it, he said, "My dad was just never around. He was always working." Under hypnosis, Ray uncovered a hidden belief that "My father isn't around because he doesn't like me." This unconscious belief had tainted Ray's relationship with his father throughout his life. Even when Ray's father attempted to get closer to him, Ray admittedly withdrew. "It just doesn't seem genuine," Ray would say.

I suggested he review memories of his father from an adult perspective, rather than through his inner child's eyes. Soon, Ray began to see the situation differently. "We had some rough times growing up, and my father put in a lot of extra hours to provide us with a comfortable life. He didn't seem to like his work, which kind of made me feel worse because I thought he was picking his job over me, and he didn't even like his job." Ray's voice began to soften. "I'm a dad now, and sometimes my job requires that I travel. I hate leaving my son, but I do it so my family can have a comfortable life. My son doesn't always understand that, and I wonder what he thinks when I leave him."

After that session, Ray began to look at his relationship with his father differently. He even went to see his dad and had a heart-to-heart conversation. Ray said, "I sat down with my dad and told him how I was worried about leaving my son so much because of my job. My father got the saddest look on his face and said he hated leaving me when I was a boy." With tears in his eyes, Ray shared how his father said, "Son, what I regret most is not having spent more quality time with you. I thought that by making enough money to buy you lots of gifts, you would realize how much I loved you. I've always felt like it did the opposite.

My only advice is that you don't make the same mistake with your son that I did with mine."

I spoke with Ray a few weeks later. He and his father were making up for the lost time. Ray said he cut back on his traveling, so the three of them (Ray, his son, and his father) could go on some fishing trips together. If Ray hadn't uncovered and updated that self-limiting belief about his father, I shudder to think of all the memories and fun they would have missed.

Many have absorbed, reinforced, and misinterpreted false ideas and paid a high emotional price. History is full of cases where crazy ideas caused terrible suffering. In France during the 1500s, thirty thousand trials were held accusing people of being werewolves! Many were found guilty and put to death. You might think that's absurd, and you'd be right, yet what beliefs are currently allowed to exist in your head that will one day seem ridiculous?

> ***"We have no say over the hand dealt us in life, but we do have a lot of control over how this hand is played."***
> Roberta Andersen

Recap

A belief is an opinion you perceive to be valid. Allowing outdated ideas from childhood, or immature remarks from others, to dictate your life is no longer an option. Even if you were pumped full of self-limiting opinions from those around you as a child, the responsibility to yank out those mental weeds and replace them with flowers (empowering beliefs) is yours alone. Kids don't have power over what happens to them, but adults do. If childish ideas are holding you back in any way, it's time to replace them and take your power back.

To eliminate an unwanted opinion, you must weaken your certainty in it by instilling doubt. Think of a belief as a round table with many supporting legs underneath. Every time you knock a leg out from beneath the table, it becomes increasingly unstable. With enough supporting legs removed, the table will collapse. Thus, the more doubt you create about the validity of the beliefs that keep you from achieving goals or being happy, the quicker those false opinions dissolve.

> ***"No one is ready for a thing until they believe they can squire it. The state of mind must be Belief, not mere hope and wish."***
> Napoleon Hill

"BELIEFS UPGRADE" EXPERIENCE

STEP 1
IDENTIFY SELF-LIMITING BELIEFS

The following written exercise will help you uncover self-limiting beliefs so you can replace them with more empowering viewpoints that cultivate inner peace and prosperity! According to the famous psychologist, Carl Jung, "Until you make the unconscious conscious, it will direct your life, and you will call it fate!"

Getting clear on what you currently believe and writing those ideas down is the first step toward creating breakthroughs in your life. Regardless of how uncomfortable your thoughts may be, write them down. Putting them to paper will make it easier to see whether these viewpoints should be supported or not moving forward. Are they kind, loving, and encouraging? Do they inspire you to do better or reach a fuller potential?

It will also allow you to look back on previously held beliefs to see how they were leading to unsatisfactory results. You can also chart how much progress you've made over the next few weeks. With that said, let's get started.

INSTRUCTIONS

Write down what you currently believe, and are telling yourself, about the topics below. Be honest and avoid filtering your thoughts. If you need more room, use a separate notebook or journal. Ignore the *_______________? for now.

For example, under How Do I View Myself, others have written:

1. I'm not smart enough to figure out how to get my life/weight/finances where I want them to be.
2. I love myself, but I don't like myself because my life is a mess.
3. I've failed so many times, maybe I don't deserve to feel good about myself.

How Would I Describe The World Around Me?

1. Life is unfair and cruel.
2. You can't trust people and they will only let you down.
3. I can't be my true self because my family will reject me.

MY CURRENT (NEGATIVE) SELF-LIMITING BELIEFS

How Do I View Myself?

1. ______________________________

2. ______________________________

3. ______________________________

*According to ____________________?

How Would I Describe The World Around Me?

1. ______________________________

2. ______________________________

3. ______________________________

*According to ______________ ?

What Do I Believe About My Appearance?

1. ______________________________

2. ______________________________

3. ______________________________

*According to ______________ ?

What Do I Believe About My Confidence?

1. ______________________________

2. ______________________________

3. ______________________________

*According to ______________ ?

What Are My Beliefs About Money?

1. ______________________________

2. ______________________________

3. ______________________________

*According to ____________________?

What Are My Beliefs About Relationships?

1. ______________________________

2. ______________________________

3. ______________________________

*According to ____________________?

What Are My Beliefs About Achieving Goals?

1. ______________________________

2. ______________________________

3. ______________________________

*According to ____________________?

What Are My Beliefs About Being Financially Abundant?

1. ______________________________

2. ______________________________

3. ______________________________

*According to ______________ ?

The following are common self-limiting beliefs:

"I'm not good enough."
"I'm not worthy."
"I can't do it."
"I don't know how."
"Things will never work out for me."
"I'll fail."
"I'll get rejected."
"Relationships are painful."
"I'll always be broke."
"There's never enough."
"I can't achieve my goals."
"The world is cruel."
"All I have is bad luck."
"People will leave me."
"I'm not smart enough."
"It's too late."
"All my opportunities have passed me by."
"I'm too fat and nobody would want me."
"I'll always be alone."

Did you write down any of that fear-based BS? (Belief Systems)

Now, go back to each of those self-limiting opinions and answer the question of **according to* ?*" "I'm not good enough ***according to whom?*"** Dad? Mom? Childhood friends? A teacher from sixth grade who made a silly comment that got stuck in your head? Are YOU reinforcing this fearful idea because you've had experiences that support this notion? Did you ever think you had those past experiences *BECAUSE* this fearful belief was unconsciously causing you to act that way, and not because the belief is accurate? You weren't born with limiting beliefs. Somewhere along the line, you learned how to deal with adversity by observing how those around you handled it. Or, you picked up false beliefs about yourself because you incorrectly interpreted situations from the past to mean something that was false. It's time to re-build your belief system as an adult, and not from the perspective of a child. Let's continue knocking out the legs from underneath this outdated table of beliefs, so they crumble down. Then, we will build a new set of prosperous beliefs that will strengthen you and transform your quality of life! Remember, you are only *one belief* away from creating tremendous breakthroughs in any and all areas of life! Go back and add the *according to (whom)? Then continue reading. You got this!

STEP 2
BELIEFS UPGRADE

Mike came in for help to quit smoking. He drove a truck for a living and said he'd tried everything to stop but was up to four packs of cigarettes a day. "I smoke all the time to stay awake and cope with boredom. I'll have one (cigarette) in my mouth, one in the tray, and I'll catch myself going to light another one. I don't know if hypnosis will help me. It doesn't seem like anything ever works out for me."

Did you catch Mike's limiting belief at the end? *"It doesn't seem like anything ever works out for me."* I led him through the first of our two sessions and told him to do his best.

Two days later, Mike returned and was visibly upset. I asked how he was doing, and he blurted out, "I blew it! I know it's my fault. I'm so mad at myself."

I told him things would be all right and asked how much he had smoked. He said, "I had one."

I said, "You had one cigarette every five minutes or every hour?"

"No, I just had one."

I sat back in my chair and smiled. "Mike, are you telling me you've only had *one* cigarette in the last two days? You cut out 159 cigarettes from your routine, and that's a failure? No way! That's an A in any classroom in America."

He paused. "Huh, I never looked at it that way. I figured if I smoked, I blew it. But when you say it like that, I guess I've done a pretty good job."

I smiled broadly. "You certainly did. Now we only have one tiny cigarette to get rid of, and you are all set."

He smiled back and said, "Hell, that will be easy. I just wish I had talked to you before putting myself through all this grief the last couple of days."

Mike did put down that last cigarette and hasn't smoked since. It was possible because we upgraded his self-sabotaging belief that nothing ever worked out for him. We used a tool called the Beliefs Upgrade to reinforce two things. First, things *do* work out for him, because they just did. Second, being supportive of oneself, especially during difficult times, is the way to go.

The Beliefs Upgrade is a series of five questions that prove or disprove a belief. It also clarifies the pros and cons of supporting various opinions and helps you upgrade viewpoints that hold you back.

Mike took his self-limiting belief that "Nothing ever works out for me" through the Beliefs Upgrade, and this is what happened.

MIKE'S INITIAL BELIEF: "NOTHING EVER WORKS OUT FOR ME."

1. **Is this idea absolute truth (a fact) or an opinion?** In other words, has absolutely nothing ever worked out for you before? Like, you never learned how to speak, walk, dress, drive, or read?

   Mike's answer: "It's an opinion. Many things have worked out for me in the past."

2. **Does this opinion do anything to improve the quality of your life?**

   Mike's answer: "No. It only causes me to downplay my accomplishments."

3. **If this idea is false, how will your life be different or better?**

   Mike's answer: "I would feel more confident about taking chances and bettering my life. I've had opportunities, but I've always let them go, even when I knew I could do a good job. I'm going to start going for things and then see what happens. My family will be happier, and I'll feel a lot better about myself."

4. **If you could believe anything, and *you can*, what belief would you rather support instead? *(What's the opposite of the fear-based opinion?)***

   Mike's answer: "Things *do* work out for me, and I'm worth believing in."

5. **How will life be better now by supporting your new belief?**

   Mike's answer: "I'm not going to drive a truck for the rest of my life. Driving has been good, don't get me wrong, but I don't want to be on the road forever. Actually, my supervisor was just telling me to apply for a new management position. I've been blowing him off, but now, I'm going to see what happens. After all, things work out for me, right."

Now that you've seen how we upgraded Mike's self-limiting belief using the Beliefs Upgrade, it's time to apply it to beliefs holding you back. Return to the statements you wrote down in Step 1 about your self-confidence, money, relationships, etc., and take any fear-based or negative beliefs about those topics through the five questions. In doing so, you'll create more empowering opinions for Step 3.

1. Is this idea absolute truth (a fact) or an opinion?
2. Does this opinion do anything to improve the quality of your life?
3. If this idea is false, how will your life be different or better?
4. If you could believe anything, and *you can*, what belief would you rather support instead? (What is the opposite of the outdated opinion?)
5. How will life improve now by supporting your new belief?

Self-limiting ideas create a chain reaction of events that seem to provide evidence for the belief itself. I used to think I had no musical ability because I couldn't play an instrument. If I looked at sheet music and couldn't read it or attempted to play something on a piano and it sounded horrible, I took this as "proof" that I didn't have the musical gene. Of course, I had never taken music lessons or put serious time into learning how to play the piano, so my assumption that I had zero musical talent was nonsense. I just didn't have the training. Yet, your mind will seek out evidence to prove whatever you already believe. Often, Democrats and Republicans walk away with the same beliefs and viewpoints they started with when negotiating or debating. Neither side seeks to understand the other but to prove only why their party is on the right side of the truth.

Weakening Fear

When Mike upgraded his beliefs, his behaviors improved, which allowed him to achieve his goal and strengthen the new view of himself. One of the tools I used to help him accomplish this is laughter. Laughing is one of the fastest and most enjoyable ways to enter a more resourceful state of mind. Therefore, the next time a negative thought comes up, yell aloud, "What a bunch of BS!"

For example:

"I can't do anything right. **What a bunch of BS!**"
"I'm not worthy. **What a bunch of BS!**"
"I can't figure this out. **What a bunch of BS!**"

Those are just lousy opinions (**B**elief **S**ystems), and you have the power to upgrade all of them right now. Return to your list of current beliefs, and after each one that's fear-based or critical, write down, "What a bunch of BS!" You'll soon be looking back at those ideas thinking they are as accurate as you being a werewolf. Once you've accomplished this task, continue reading. Do this now.

Great! Now read the following sentence out loud: **"Those outdated ideas are BS, and I'm no longer willing to tolerate that nonsense. I deserve better, and every day, in every way, I am getting better and better!"**

You may think these statements are a little cheesy. But laughter counteracts fear and self-doubt, and there's nothing corny about having the guts to stand up to your deepest fears. When one admits out loud, "I feel like a failure," it can be the first step toward erasing that belief. Great, you feel like a failure; I've felt that way too. Yet, there is no failure, only feedback. You have plenty of feedback about what choices are helpful and hurtful. What are you going to do with that feedback moving forward?" Use that question to build a more empowering future.

STEP 3
YOUR NEW BELIEFS

It's time to return to the Beliefs Upgrade tool and pull out the new, more empowering beliefs from Question 4 that you'd rather support instead from now on! Write down your new *Prosperity* beliefs in the space provided!

NEW PROSPERITY BELIEFS

How I View Myself Now.

1. ______________________________

2. ______________________________

3. ______________________________

How I Describe The World Around Me Now.

1. ______________________________

2. ______________________________

3. ______________________________

What I Believe About My Appearance Now.

1. ______________________________

2. ______________________________

3. ______________________________

What I Believe About My Confidence Now.

1. ______________________________

2. ______________________________

3. ______________________________

What I Believe About Money Now.

1. ______________________________

2. ______________________________

3. ______________________________

What I Believe About Relationships Now.

1. ______________________________

2. ______________________________

3. ______________________________

What I Believe About Achieving Goals Now.

1. ______________________________

2. ______________________________

3. ______________________________

What I Believe About Being Financially Abundant Now.

1. ____

2. ____

3. ____

STEP 4
DAILY STRENGTHENING

Now that you've identified your new **Prosperity Beliefs**, it's time to strengthen them through reinforcement.

Over the next 21 days, say each Prosperity Belief ten times out loud to yourself when you first wake up, and another ten times right before going to sleep. During those times, your mind is most open to suggestion, which is why you should never fall asleep in front of the television!

You can further strengthen the new opinions you've chosen for yourself by repeating these beliefs while walking, exercising, listening to your favorite song, driving in the car, or giving yourself a big hug as you smile in the mirror. Remember, receiving suggestions while in an emotionally or physically energized state drives the ideas deeper into your mental hard drive.

If you'd like an even more powerful experience, visit **www.SurvivingToThriving.me** and take advantage of the companion course. It comes with audio coaching lessons and a hypnosis audio program for reinforcing your Prosperity Mindset. You'll find yourself feeling more self-assured, energetic, peaceful, and prosperous than ever before.

PROSPERITY LIST

You'll be creating new Prosperity Beliefs throughout this journey. I've created space at the end of this book to put all your Prosperity Beliefs in one place for daily reinforcement.

Examples Of Empowering Beliefs

"I am more than enough!"

"I am awesome, and I help others feel awesome too!"

"I'm looking and feeling better every day!"

"I love myself and my body and invest in taking care of me each day!"

"I have strong confidence and self-worth!"

"I am worthy of love, acceptance, respect, happiness, and care."

"I enjoy loving, connected relationships with others."

"I bring value to the lives of others and always seek new ways to strengthen trust and communication."

"I set goals and achieve them because I make the pursuit enjoyable and rewarding!"

"I continually attracting money, prosperity, opportunities, and abundance into my life!"

"I always expect miracles to appear and am constantly watching for them!"

"It doesn't matter what shows up. What matters is how *I* show up, and I show up strong, confident, patient, and resourceful in all situations."

"There are lucky people in this world and I am one of them!"

CHAPTER 2
DESIGNING YOUR LIFE

"I knew that if I failed, I wouldn't regret trying.
But what I would regret is not trying."

Jeff Bezos, Founder of Amazon

For decades, people have trusted me with their deepest fears, secrets, and most desired ambitions. I've also heard enough heart-wrenching stories to fill a five hundred-page book. When you talk with a large number of people, similar themes begin emerging. One of the sentiments I heard hundreds of times was, "I don't even know who I am anymore, or what makes me happy. I've sacrificed so much of myself for others that there's nothing left of me. It's too late to do anything about it. My opportunities are long gone, and my life feels like a failure."

Almost everyone grapples with fear, regret, and the pain of loss. I've spent countless hours thinking I should have accomplished more, made better choices, acted more courageously in the past, or been more mature. These thoughts cost me many hours of sleep as I'd toss and turn while my mind reeled from past regrets and worrisome future scenarios. Through the years, I've learned to take hold of my anxious mind, redirect my awareness toward the things I have accomplished, and times when I behaved honorably. I have also trained myself to concentrate on what I'm presently grateful for and how I can continue to add value to others' lives. If a worrisome thought about the future comes to mind, I imagine what I would want to occur, and then play that out in the theatre of my imagination.

Here's how I learned to reply whenever someone said, "Who am I?" Instead of figuring out who you were, or who you are now, perhaps the better question is: **"Who do you wish to become?"** People often believe the opportunities to reach their full potential passed them by long ago, and now they have nothing ahead of them. Yet, this is a false premise. I've witnessed these same people re-discover themselves and approach life in a new way that led to incredible joy, excitement, and fulfillment. Life doesn't offer you one single chance to hit the jackpot. There are always opportunities around you, and as you actively start seeking them out, you'll start noticing them all the time.

What does the following say? **N O W H E R E**

You might have answered with "NO WHERE." Or "NOW HERE." Both are correct, depending on where you place your focus. When it comes to finding opportunities for making dreams come true, are they NO WHERE to be found, or NOW HERE? Well, that's up to you.

Let's see if this is making sense to you.

What does this say? **I M P O S S I B L E**

"IMPOSSIBLE" or "I'M POSSIBLE"?

Both are true, depending upon what you believe. As Henry Ford once remarked, "If you think you can do a thing or think you can't do a thing, you're right."

In this chapter, you will define who you want to be, instead of dwelling on who you think you are supposed to be or who you once were. For this prosperity experience, let's pretend anything is possible. Instead of feeling limited by your past or present circumstances, you are now free to dream big.

"Redefining Yourself" Experience

Answer the following questions in as much depth and detail as possible. Use the space provided to write your answers. If you need more space, grab your notebook or journal.

Step 1

1. What do you want to believe about yourself? (Now is the time to turn off your analytical brain and embrace the dreamer within.)

2. If you had a magic wand, what would you wish for and why?

3. What emotions would you like to experience more often, and what experiences produce these feelings for you?

4. What activities would you like to accomplish or experience if you had unlimited funds and time? Why?

5. If things worked out for you from now on, describe how you'd spend your days.

6. If you were to believe in yourself and your worthiness, what immediate changes would you make in life? What is the first step you'd take?

Step 2

Determine five new beliefs you would have to believe about yourself to attain and experience everything you just imagined. Take a few minutes to write your Prosperity Beliefs. It's not necessary that you wholeheartedly believe these opinions right now, just write them down so you're clear on what you want to think about yourself.

"I AM ."

"I AM ."

"I AM ."

"I AM ."

"I AM ."

Reinforcing New Beliefs

Now that you are gaining clarity about the direction in which you'd like to take your life, the next step is to get your mind to absorb and act upon the new beliefs that will get you there. Remember, your unconscious mind doesn't care what ideas you have. It's job is to take those beliefs and turn them into your reality. Thus, the following "Prosperity Upgrade" Experience will reinforce and strengthen your new beliefs at an unconscious level.

"Prosperity Upgrade" Experience

Imagine a whiteboard in your mind. This whiteboard is unique because it's linked to your unconscious mind, where self-limiting beliefs that hold you back are stored. As you sit quietly with your thoughts for a moment, imagine a self-limiting belief that's been holding you back begin to surface from your unconscious.

Allow it to appear on the whiteboard in your mind now. Write down the thought that comes to mind below.

"I   ."

Now ask yourself:

- Is this idea helping or hurting me?
- Is it allowing me to grow or keeping me stuck?
- Do I want to continue supporting this opinion?

If the belief is hurting you or keeping you stuck, imagine marching up to the whiteboard, grabbing the large eraser that's hanging there, and wiping that belief from the whiteboard. As you eliminate it from the board, it also gets deleted from your mind. If the words resist coming off, get creative and resourceful. Sometimes, these words will try to scare you into continuing to support them. They want to keep you afraid because they know if you realize you're the one with the real power, they are done. But the jig is up. *You* have the capacity, and now you know it!

If the negative statement resists fading from the whiteboard, imagine melting the board down with a flamethrower. You might even say out loud, "What a bunch of BS!" as you do so. Have you ever thrown a piece of paper into a bonfire? It quickly lights up, folds in on itself, turns into ash, and floats away. Imagine the same thing happening to the outdated belief. Do this now.

Well done! Before we move on, go back to that self-limiting belief you wrote down a moment ago and scratch it out with your pen. Then write "BS" on top of it.

Deleting negative opinions is one thing. Acting it out for real empowers you at a whole new level. If you're feeling up to the challenge, grab a separate piece of paper, write the fearful opinion down, then light the paper on fire over the sink or toilet. Rinse the ashes down the drain or flush them down the toilet with the negative energy that went with it. If you don't want to mess with fire, you can rip up the paper, toss it into a shredder, or bury it in the backyard. Use this as a ceremony for reclaiming your power.

Now take a few deep breaths through your nose and feel a sense of lightness as you slowly exhale. You are wiping the slate (whiteboard) clean, and now everything becomes possible.

Next, decide what you would rather believe about yourself instead and write it below in the space provided.

My Prosperity Belief

"I !"

Imagine grabbing a permanent marker in your favorite color, marching back up to the whiteboard in your mind, and writing the new belief in large letters across the board. (If you burned down your whiteboard with a flamethrower, imagine a clean board appearing.)

Finally, gather the other five Prosperity Beliefs you wrote at the beginning of this chapter and imagine adding them to the whiteboard. If you have challenges seeing it in your mind, talk yourself through it, or imagine what it might feel like to have the marker in your hand as you draw these words onto the whiteboard. You can also write down all six Prosperity Beliefs in the space provided at the end of this chapter.

You are providing Prosperity wishes to the part of your brain that knows how to grant them. It's the first step in using the power of your mind to create your life by design. You're becoming clear about what you want, rather than dwelling on what you don't. Gaining clarity in what you desire, and then getting more detailed about how it will look, sound, and feel when you have it, allows your reality-creating brain to start causing it to happen.

My Prosperity Beliefs

CHAPTER 3
GRANTING WISHES

"The way to get started is to quit talking and start doing."

Walt Disney

As you travel down this path, we will continually strengthen your Prosperity Beliefs while driving stress and fear into the background. Much of this journey centers on reprogramming your unconscious mind because your "mental programming" determines how happy and prosperous you are. Human beings aren't as consciously in control as we assume ourselves to be. Unconscious needs and desires from childhood drive most of the choices you make. If you wish to move from surviving to thriving, the secret is to train your brain to satisfy those unconscious needs by behaving in ways that produce the results you desire. The following experiences will help you accomplish this. But first, here's a crash course in how your mind functions.

How Your Mind Creates Reality

There are two parts of your mind with separate roles and functions that work together to create your subjective reality, in simplified terms. They are the *conscious* and *unconscious* mind. The conscious mind is the part of your brain that absorbs information through your five senses and interprets what it means based upon beliefs developed from past experiences.

The conscious mind is the logical, analytical, decision-making portion of the brain. You are using it right now to read and make sense of these words. As your eyes scan over the sentence, your analytical mind thinks, "I agree with this, and I don't agree with that." It decides what's good or evil, right or wrong, useful or threatening based upon all the experiences you've encountered in life. Your conscious mind also controls willpower. Most willpower lasts a few short minutes, and then your unconscious programming (habits) takes over.

The unconscious mind is the part of your brain that regulates autonomic bodily functions, which means it keeps your heart beating, lungs breathing, and blood circulating without any conscious effort. Keeping you alive isn't the only thing your unconscious mind does without your voluntary consent. Most of the thoughts, feelings, and actions you experience are also on autopilot, which means your brain is continually making decisions on handling situations without your permission. Like Robert Ripley used to say, "Believe it or not!"

In a groundbreaking study, neuroscientists at the Max Planck Institute for Human Cognitive and Brain Sciences found that many of our so-called conscious decisions are made by the unconscious mind seven seconds before we become aware of them. In the experiment, participants could freely decide to press a button with their left or right hand. The only stipulation was they had to remember *when* they made the decision to use their left or right hand.

Using fMRI, researchers scanned the brains of participants during the study to determine if they could predict which hand participants would use *before* they were consciously aware of their decision. By monitoring the micro patterns of activity in the frontopolar cortex, the researchers successfully predicted which hand participants would choose a full seven seconds before the participant was aware of their own decision.

John-Dylan Haynes, a Max Planck Institute neuroscientist and co-author of the study, said, "Unconscious brain activity heavily influences your decisions. By the time consciousness kicks in, most of the work is already complete." Think about the last time something flew toward your face, and you flinched. Whether it was a bug or a family member throwing a pillow at your head, your nervous system reacted to the incoming stimulus before you could process what was happening consciously. Whether you call it a reflex, habit, or mental programming, your unconscious mind has a tremendous influence over your life. Why not use that to your advantage.

If you are married, you've probably had the same argument about a particular topic a hundred times. You can likely recite what your partner says and how you respond verbatim. You might even tell yourself, "I'm not going to react that way the next time," but then return to the same response you always go to and wonder how that's possible. It's because your good intentions are stored in your conscious mind, and not reinforced at an unconscious level. When the old pattern (argument) occurs again, your brain activates the original program stored in your unconscious mind (fight, deflect, defend, or flee). The solution is to program new responses to old situations into your unconscious mind.

Most recurring arguments aren't spurred because of what's happening at the moment. Instead, certain behaviors push buttons (emotional reactions) that formed in childhood. As your unconscious mind developed survival strategies for managing life, a set of mental rules became established for how things should be. When these unconscious rules get violated, we feel emotionally threatened and react accordingly. Famous author and personal development coach, Tony Robbins, once shared the "Rules for Happiness" on the *Larry King Live* show. He said, "If what you think *should* be happening in your life equals what *is* happening, you are happy. If what you think *should* be happening *isn't* happening, you will feel unhappy. If you think what *should* be happening *isn't* happening, and you believe *you can't do anything to change it*, you become depressed."

The key ingredients are what you think *should* be happening and the belief of whether you are *capable* of improving your situation. Often, the fastest way to happiness is by releasing your "shoulds," which means updating your mental rules if they are causing unhappiness or frustration in your life. Instead of thinking you should be forty pounds lighter before being happy, you could decide to be happy now while pursuing your goal. I've helped thousands of people comfortably lose weight and keep it off without dieting, and those who worked on being more joyful and loving to themselves each day lost weight faster and easier than those who didn't. Those who chose to love and accept themselves before losing the weight were also able to remain in a happy, healthy, right-sized body, rather than to relapse. That was possible because they upgraded their mental rules around self-worth and emotional eating. If you're interested in learning those new rules that lead to exciting and sustainable weight loss, get my book, *Losing Weight Without Losing Your Mind!* (www.LoseWeightEasier.com)

Rather than believing your spouse should respond the way you want him/her to, you could choose to accept and appreciate all his/her other traits you admire. When you bring peaceful, loving energy to the relationship, your connection will improve significantly rather than being upset or blaming your partner for your unhappiness. Couples who've been happily married for decades will tell you the secret is to "blow things off." Don't make mountains out of molehills. Dr. Phil once said it this way: "You can be right or happy. Choose wisely." It doesn't mean you ignore problems that need addressing. Instead, it's how you address those issues that determine whether they get resolved quickly and in an empowering way or not. Patience, straightforwardness, and kindness produce much better outcomes when asking for what you need, than yelling, ignoring, or defending.

The good news is you can condition your unconscious mind to respond automatically in positive, proactive ways. When I write about training your brain for success, I'm referring to this.

YOUR INNER GENIE

Think of your unconscious as a genie that lives in the back of your brain. Two things determine what wishes your internal genie grants. First, the beliefs you hold about yourself, others, and the world around you. Second, what you focus on and repetitively say to yourself most of the time. Even though beliefs heavily influence people, it is possible to override the system with your conscious thoughts. Your genie is always watching the movies, images, and memories you keep alive in the theatre of your imagination and eavesdropping on the conversation you have with yourself. Whatever it sees or hears you say the most, the assumption is that's what you want, and your genie begins manifesting it.

The thoughts you hold in your mind's privacy, if held long enough and backed up by strong emotion, will eventually produce outcomes in your life that reflect those ideas. In other words, what you think about comes about.

Have you ever heard of a self-fulfilling prophecy? It's a granted wish. Self-fulfilling prophecies occur when you repeatedly tell yourself something is going to happen, and it does. But the blind spot is you don't realize you're the one who set it into motion. People unknowingly talk themselves into experiencing what they don't want because they keep concentrating on those thoughts and feelings. When the fearful situation occurs, you say, "See, I told you this would happen," not realizing you are responsible for either creating or attracting it into your life. Imagine driving down a road, and your car starts to swerve. There's nothing to run into except a telephone poll one hundred feet away on the other side of the roadway. You start telling yourself, "Just don't hit the pole. Just don't hit the pole." A few seconds later, you crash right into the pole because that's where your attention was focused. Your inner genie has difficulty processing negation. It has a hard time "not" doing something, and it also tends to ignore the word "don't." What it hears is, "Just ~~don't~~ hit the pole!" What should you say instead? "Just stay on the road!"

You may have heard of the Law of Attraction. It states that what you think about most, and feel with emotion, you draw (attract) into your life. On December 7, 1941, Earl Nightingale was at Pearl Harbor, standing in a lookout tower on the Battleship Arizona. A thousand men died on the ship that day, and Earl was one of only a hundred who survived. Earl felt God spared his life for a reason. After the war, he became obsessed with why so many in his neighborhood were poor and struggling. When two people start with similar backgrounds, why was one person able to create wealth and happiness for his family, while the other stayed stagnant and broke? Answering these questions became Earl's life work.

He began spending more time reading about successful people and took a job working first in radio and then in the insurance business. Everywhere he went, he sought out successful people to mentor him. Eventually, Earl acquired enough knowledge and experience to create his insurance agency. In 1956, he prepared to take a trip but wanted to leave words of encouragement for his salesforce. That night, he awoke with a message of inspiration to share with his team in the morning. That message became one of the most potent and famous motivational recordings ever made. Earl Nightingale later turned this into a book entitled, *The Strangest Secret.* He said, "The strangest secret is that whatever you focus on most of the time, your life becomes!"

My question for you is, "What are you spending most of your time focusing on?" I hope it's centered around all the things you want to experience in life, and not on "hitting the pole." People unconsciously initiate useful and un-useful self-fulfilling prophecies all the time. Once you understand how self-fulfilling prophecies function, you can intentionally use them to your advantage. Your genie (unconscious mind) doesn't think about what's good or bad for you in the long run. That's the function of your conscious mind. Your genie follows orders. That's why it's crucial that you focus on what you want and fill your head with thoughts that converge around the outcomes you desire.

> *"When willpower is matched against imagination, imagination always prevails."*
> Albert Einstein

"GRANTING WISHES" EXPERIENCE

Even when convinced that all your emotional or psychological wounds are healed, you'll come across an obstacle that has another self-limiting belief fueling it sooner or later. You've already learned powerful ways to upgrade self-limiting beliefs, yet I want you to have several tools in your toolbox, so here's one more.

Imagine your unconscious mind uses a filing system to organize your beliefs, habits, and emotional responses. It contains folders within this system that store things you "like," and things you "dislike." For instance, if you enjoy eating broccoli, that bit of information would be stored in the "like" folder. If you think Brussels sprouts are gross, that idea would be kept in the "dislike" folder.

There are many types of folders within this cataloging system, including ones for judgments you believe are "true" and "false." A quick way to install a positive self-fulfilling prophecy is by moving a self-limiting belief from the "true" folder into the "false" folder. As soon as you believe in something you didn't before, or no longer buy into something you used to think was so, the mental block disappears. For example, if you think you can't do something, and then suddenly believe you can, you'll take action in a new way that produces the desired outcome.

I've helped thousands of people move the sabotaging belief that "I'm not worthy of being loved" into the "false" folder of their mind. We'd concurrently transfer the "I am worthy, and I love myself," belief into their "true" folder. Immediately, clients would begin caring affectionately for themselves and trusting the intentions of others more. You can have the same experience. Use the following exercise to move your self-limiting beliefs into the "false" folder and more empowering beliefs into your mind's "true" folder.

To begin, let's figure out whether you are more visual (see pictures in your mind's eye), auditory (prefer listening to audiobooks rather than reading them), or kinesthetic (operate off of gut feelings and are a hands-on kind of person).

Think of something you know with absolute certainty is false. If you're a female, it might be, "My name is Frank." How do you know this statement is false? Do you see a picture of it in your mind that seems blurred or hazy? Do you hear a voice in your head that says, "I don't think so?" Or do you get an uneasy feeling in a part of your body (e.g., stomach) that signals this is false? Pay attention to what's happening in your mind and body to decipher how you know something is incorrect. Imagine someone telling you something that you know is false. Notice how your mind and body let you know this data is inaccurate.

Once, when asking a client to identify how he knew something was false, whether he pictured it, heard it, or felt it, he said, "It's just illogical." He verified his disbelief using an auditory response. When presented with inaccurate information, he would tell himself it was illogical using a matter-of-fact tone. For him, his tone of voice confirmed the data should be in his "false" folder.

If you are feeling a bit confused right now, that's okay. I am helping you make an unconscious process become conscious. Unless you've invested a lot of time into developing self-awareness, you might not be tuned in to the signals your mind and body are consistently sending you. Eventually, you'll understand how all of this fits together, and when that happens, you'll be blown away by the immense power of this "Granting Wishes" Experience.

Here's one more example to help this exercise make more sense. I recommend rereading these examples a couple of times to decipher better how *your* mind sorts out the truth from fiction.

Cynthia came to see me because she was frustrated with her income and had struggled to get a promotion at work. I told her about the "Granting Wishes" Experience and then asked her to think of something she knew was false. As I watched her eyes, she glanced up and over to her right and said, "I have two dogs." I jotted down, *"False Folder"—up and over to her right.*

Then I said, "Now, tell me something true." She glanced over to her left and said, "I have one dog." I then wrote down, *"True Folder"—over to her left.* I asked, "When you think of having two dogs, how do you know this is false?" She replied, "I see a small black and white picture of my dog and an empty space next to him." Underneath the previous note for Cynthia's "False Folder," I wrote, *Black and white picture with space.*

I asked, "When you think of the true statement, how do you imagine it?" She said, "I see a big colorful picture of my dog," as she glanced again to her left. Thus, I added, *Big, colorful picture* to the description of her "True Folder."

This brief conversation revealed precisely how Cynthia's brain sorted whether she believed something was accurate or not. Her "false" folder was up and to her right, and when she felt something was wrong, she unconsciously turned it into "a small black and white picture with an empty space" in her mind. Cynthia did the exact opposite with her "true" folder. The truthful image was a big, colorful picture over to her left.

Why is this information so useful? Because knowing how your brain naturally stores information gives you the ability to strengthen or weaken any idea (and feeling) instantly by putting it in the correct folder.

I then took Cynthia through the "Awakening" Experience to discover the precise belief that was blocking her ability to attain greater prosperity. You'll have the opportunity to encounter this in the coming chapters. As it turned out, Cynthia felt unworthy of getting the promotion because she didn't have a college education, and others in her company did. This limiting belief of not being educated enough created tremendous conflict within her.

Even though she didn't have a degree, Cynthia worked harder and brought in more new clients than anyone else in her office.

We took the belief that she was "unworthy," which her mind stored as "a color picture on her left side" (in the "true" folder) and moved it over to her right (into the "false" folder). Then she changed the image to "black and white" since that's how she imaged inaccurate data. I asked how she felt about the unworthy belief now that it's in her "false" folder, and she replied, "Give me a minute."

Her eyes squinted as she looked to her right, and then all at once, her demeanor changed. She took a deep breath in, softened her shoulders, and relaxed into the chair. Then she looked at me and said, "Sorry about that. I started feeling better, but not all the way, so I made the picture smaller, and all of a sudden, I felt this incredible sense of freedom come over me!"

I smiled and said, "Great! Now let's take it one step further. Tell me what you want to believe about yourself instead." She replied, "I do deserve a promotion because I'm worth it, and I bring tremendous value to my company!" I said, "Then make a large color picture of yourself getting a raise and place it over to your left" (because that's where her "true" folder was located). She took a few minutes to do so, and a broad smile appeared on her face.

The following week, Cynthia strolled into my office, grinning from ear to ear. "How are you today?" I asked. She replied, "Great! After our last session, I felt so good about myself that I went right up to my boss the next day and asked for that promotion. I even asked for the exact amount I imagined getting. He was a little resistant at first, but I knew he didn't want to lose me, so he gave it to me! The funny thing is, he didn't mention anything about my not having a degree. I wish I would have asked for this a long time ago, but I have it now!"

Who would have thought that moving pictures around in your mind could have such profound and immediate results, yet it does. Now let's put it to work for you.

Step 1: Identify the Belief You Wish to Change

Write down the self-limiting belief (fear) you want to make false in your head, so it doesn't hold you back any longer.

Step 2: Classify Your "False" and "True" Folders

Use the following questions to identify your "false" folder's characteristics and then write your answers below so you can remember them for later.

1. Create an image in your mind of something you know is false. Do you see a picture, hear a sound, or feel something when you imagine this incorrect data?

2. If it's a picture, where is it located in your personal space? Is it in front of you, to the left, to the right, up close, or far away? Is it in color or black and white? Is it a large, medium, or small image?

3. If you don't see a picture, perhaps you hear a sound. I had a client say that whenever he thought of something false, he'd listen to a sarcastic voice in the back of his mind say, "Not!" Notice the details. For him, it was a mocking voice that originated from the back of his head.

4. If you don't see a picture or hear a sound, perhaps you get a feeling. When you think of something false, what kind of sensations do you get? Where do you sense its location in your body? I've had clients say when something felt false, they had a rock in their stomach. Again, pay attention to the details (rock, stomach).

5. Write down below what you see, hear, and feel when something is false. You may want to use your smartphone to video yourself while thinking about this. Observe what direction your eyes move in or notice how you suddenly shift your facial expression or body.

"FALSE" FOLDER

____

____

____

____

____

____

The next step is to use the following questions to identify your "true" folder's characteristics and then write down your answers so you can remember them for later.

1. Create an image in your mind of something you know is true. Do you see a picture, hear a sound, or get a feeling when you imagine this incorrect data?
2. If it's a picture, where is it located in your personal space? Is it in front of you, to the left, to the right, up close, or far away? Is it in color or black and white? Is it a large, medium, or small image?
3. If you don't see a picture, perhaps you hear a sound. Do you listen to a voice inside of your head? What kind of tone does it have? Is it loud, soft, reassuring, or matter of fact? Is the sound or voice coming from the front,

side, center, or back of your mind? When something is correct, is it quiet in your head?

4. If you don't see a picture or hear a sound, maybe you get a feeling. When you think of something false, what kind of sensations do you get? Is there a relaxed sensation? Is your breathing slower and more rooted in your chest? Are there other vibrations in your body? Where?
5. Write down what you see, hear, and feel when something is true. You may want to use your smartphone to video yourself while thinking about this. Observe what direction your eyes move in or notice how you suddenly shift your facial expression or body.

"TRUE" FOLDER

Note: Occasionally, clients will say their false and true files are in the same location. If you continue examining more of the attributes (size, area, shape, volume, texture, distance, etc.), you should notice distinctions, even if they are slight.

STEP 3: ELIMINATE FEAR-BASED IDEAS

Now the fun part! It's time to take the self-limiting fear you wrote down in Step 1 and move it into the "false" folder.

1. Imagine taking the fear-based belief out of the "true" folder and moving it into the "false" folder. Then, modify the self-limiting belief characteristics, so it matches the features listed for the "false" folder in Step 2.
2. Remember the example with Cynthia and her dog? Images in her "false" folder were "black and white and had empty spaces." Use the criteria you wrote down and modify how you think of that old, outdated belief now.
3. Next, test the change by thinking of the self-limiting belief and notice if the feelings have shifted. It should feel different—maybe neutral, indifferent, or like complete nonsense. It might now feel foreign or silly to think you used to buy into that stinking thinking.

STEP 4: STRENGTHEN DESIRED BELIEFS

Finally, write down the new, more empowering belief (wish) you want to feel with total certainty is true about you!

"I AM ______________________________________!"

1. Imagine taking the desired belief out of the "false" folder and move it into the "true" folder. Then modify the characteristics of the desired belief, so it matches the features listed for the "true" folder in Step 2.
2. Now test it by thinking of the new, empowering opinion and notice how it now feels more believable and accurate. You may want to increase the brightness of the image and move it closer, make it sound more convincing, and attach a warm feeling. Use your imagination

to play around with your new belief's attributes until it feels just the way you want.

As you continue recognizing how your brain stores information, you'll quickly add and delete beliefs, fears, and bad habits using this wish-granting formula. Your brain is extraordinary, and so are you!

CHAPTER 4

COMFORTABLE BEING UNCOMFORTABLE

"If everything seems under control, you're just not going fast enough!"

Mario Andretti, legendary race car driver

Feeling comfortable is a basic human need, but it can also hold you back from experiencing your full potential. Push-ups can feel uncomfortable, yet through doing them, you'll become physically strong and healthier. Problems, obstacles, and circumstances that block you from quickly attaining your goals are emotionally uncomfortable. However, through finding ways to solve those predicaments, you become more resilient and wiser.

Part of your personal and spiritual development is to learn how to feel more comfortable being uncomfortable because it will accelerate your growth. One of the most common self-sabotages is trading in long-term results for immediate gratification. As soon as attempting to follow through on a task starts to feel hard, most cave in and quit. Even when there is physical or emotional discomfort, the ones who don't stop make significant gains and turn their goals into realities. Therefore, the next step in this journey is to strengthen mental toughness by expanding your comfort zone.

Let's start by testing the boundaries of your current comfort zone. The instructions for this exercise are simple. Sing out loud right now: "We are the champions, my friend. And we'll be together until the end." (*Try hitting the high notes like Freddy Mercury from the band, Queen!*) Ready, SING! "We are the champions, my friend. And we'll be together until the end."

Did you sing it? If so, great! I'm proud of you. If not, here's another chance. Sing these words as loud as you can, and if others are around, sing even louder. Let's see how courageous you are. Here you go. 1, 2, 3! "We are the champions, my friend. And we'll be together until the end."

Great! Give yourself a round of applause for following through, especially if it made you uncomfortable, and you did it anyway.

If you still haven't sung this tune, why not?

- Was it too silly for you?
- Are you too dignified?
- Afraid someone might judge you?
- Are you in a rush to get to the next exercise?
- Did you feel embarrassed?
- Are you too busy analyzing my intentions instead of following the instructions or trusting your guide on this journey?

The only reason I asked you to sing out loud was to see if you would do it. This test reveals how well you deal with challenges and how willing you are to leave or expand your comfort zone. It also says something about your coachability and how well you follow instructions. If you completed the task by singing aloud, you are willing to take risks to grow and reap the rewards.

If you did not take action as requested, even after getting a second (and third) chance, it implies you don't take many risks, are overly concerned with how others might judge you, or you need to follow instructions better. You may justify your actions by thinking the test is stupid, unnecessary, or not that big of a deal. However, realize that's your ego getting in the way. Excuses, regardless of where they originate from, hold people back from attaining the goals they desire. Action creates momentum, progress, and achievement. Excuses and justifications lead to anger, self-pity, and stagnation.

As a kid, I didn't like homework and would find any excuse not to do it. My grades were average at best, and instead of realizing it was directly related to my not studying, I assumed I wasn't smart and that studying was a waste of time. My mother's and teachers' disapproval only made me feel worse about it, which deepened my procrastination. I was a C student in high school, and guidance counselors said I would never get into college with my grades. Yet, whenever someone told me I couldn't do something, I'd think, *Watch me!*

I did get into college, perhaps just to prove my advisors wrong, and had to take remedial math and English classes to graduate. It was embarrassing, but not enough to change my behavior around studying. Pain doesn't change behavior, and often fuels us to cling to poor coping strategies even more! I felt stupid doing homework because I had a hard time remembering what I'd learned and getting poor grades on exams only reinforced in my mind that I wasn't a smart person.

During my senior year of college, an advisor told me I would not get into graduate school because of my grades. I thought, *Watch me!* and got into a graduate school on probation. I had to take a couple of extra courses, and that's when it happened. I realized that instead of making up excuses for not doing the work, I just needed to do it and get out of my comfort zone. That's when the breakthrough happened. I began studying every single night and during the day on Saturdays and Sundays. My GPA went from a 2.4 to a 3.5, and test-taking became easier. I started feeling smart for the first time in my life and began enjoying studying more. Eventually, it became a habit. I've been "doing my daily homework" ever since, and I no longer make excuses for not following through on actions that produce successful outcomes.

> ***"Your biggest breakthroughs are hidden in the places you don't want to go!"***
> Tim Shurr

You cannot grow if you're playing it safe. Your goal is to become more comfortable with being uncomfortable. Decide that it's okay to feel weird or unsure during challenging periods of growth because the rewards are worth it. You can't have courage without also being afraid, and only in times of great adversity can your inner hero emerge. The next time you're called upon to take action, follow Nike's slogan and "Just do it!"

COMFORT ZONE VS. QUICKSAND

Each time you find yourself procrastinating on goal-attaining activities, be aware of the excuses that enter your mind for not taking action. Write them down because they will lead you to the unconscious belief(s) responsible for sabotaging the results you could be experiencing.

COMFORT ZONE STATEMENTS (EXCUSES)

"I don't have enough time."
"I don't have any money."
"I'm too tired."
"I have no willpower."
"It's my (parents'/spouse's/job's/economy's) fault."
"I don't know how."
"It won't last, so why bother."
"It won't work out anyway."
"I don't feel like it."
"I don't have any resources."

"Now's not a good time."
"I have too many commitments."
"I have to take care of my parents."
"Nobody listens to me (or takes me seriously)."
"My spouse isn't supportive."
"I'm selfish if I take care of myself."

Write Down Quicksand (Comfort) Statement You Commonly Use:

1.

2.

3.

4.

5.

6.

7.

8.

9.

10.

Next, imagine having unshakeable confidence and unwavering faith in yourself and your abilities. You also have access to all the resources in the world for making dreams come true. From this empowered point of view, how would you positively respond to each of those excuses? If you are a person of faith, you can also imagine how God would think of those statements.

Go back to the comfort zone statements you just wrote down, and underneath each one, write a more empowering declaration. (Hint: Jot down the opposite of what's there.)

For example:

"I don't have enough time."

I have enough time, and I make time for the most important things. I'm getting better at prioritizing my schedule every day!

"I don't have any resources."

I have all the resources needed to make my dreams come true, and I'm getting better at recognizing and using them every day!

If you have difficulty coming up with empowering statements, call an upbeat friend, and ask them how they would respond to the following comments. You can also search for Google solutions, post the question in an online forum, or listen to my podcast (MesmerizingPodcast.com). In doing so, you'll be tapping into the resources God has already placed in your life to help you grow and excel.

The moment you start looking for solutions is the moment they begin appearing!

Daily Stretching Produces Flexibility

Because you are amazing, here's another opportunity to expand your comfort zone! Instead of singing, say the following out loud as you gently use your middle finger to tap on the center of your forehead: "I have the power to create my destiny!"

Continue tapping your forehead with your finger, as if you're driving this affirmation deep into your unconscious mind. Passionately recite the empowering statements below out loud, emphasizing the italicized words as you do so:

> "*I* have the power to create my destiny!!"
> "I have the *power* to create my destiny!"
> "I have the power to create *my* destiny!"
> "I have the power to create my *destiny*!"

Fantastic! I know you stepped up this time. Since transformation requires new information and action, it's normal to feel resistant when first making changes. Encouraging you to sing out loud may seem like it has nothing to do with creating inner peace and prosperity. Yet, as you will see, it has *everything* to do with it.

These courage-creating exercises reveal your current levels of comfort, inner security, and confidence, and as you progress through the experiences along this journey, these levels will all increase.

"We've Always Done It This Way!"

When first taking my psychological tools for building higher-performing teams into corporate America, I was surprised by how many company leaders clung to outdated ideas that held back their organization and team members' growth. Of course, they didn't realize the resistance to new ideas had become a blind spot that was halting their growth. Most wanted to keep the status quo because their approach had produced success for them in the past, and they didn't want to lose their mojo. Yet, what happens in business is like what happens in nature. If you're not growing, you're dying. You must continue learning and adapting to remain fruitful, prosperous, and sustainable.

Comfort zones aren't always comfortable, but they are familiar, and it causes us to dig in when we should be letting go. I once heard about an eight-year-old who complained of organizing the recyclables and taking them out to the curb. The boy's mother was strict and demanded he sorts the newspapers, glass, and plastics into separate containers. One day the boy was late in getting the recyclables to the street. He ran out with three different boxes just as the recycling truck pulled up. Shocked, the boy watched as the driver emptied the containers of newspapers, glass, and plastics all into one big pile in the back of the recycling truck. Excitedly, he ran to share the news with his mother.

However, she met his enthusiasm with cold disbelief and instructed him to continue sorting as usual. The following week when the recyclable truck pulled up, the boy begged his mother to watch the man through the window. Reluctantly, she agreed and saw with her own eyes as the man dumped the newspapers, glass, and plastics into one big pile. The boy beamed with satisfaction, expecting his mother to make amends. Instead, she looked at her son and said, "It doesn't matter. We've always done it this way, and we are going to continue doing it this way. That's just how it is."

How do you think the boy interpreted the thought processes of his mother?

"Don't trust what you see."

"Do what you've always done even if it doesn't make sense."

"Don't question things."

"Life is unfair. That's just how it is."

I bet you know someone who's behaved similarly. People come up with all kinds of rituals for how things should be because it makes them feel safe or in control. I attended a Lutheran graduate school while working on my master's degree in psychology. One day, I approached a respected professor of religious studies with a question. "Professor, why do some people with strict religious views refuse to listen to anything that challenges their beliefs?" He said, "These people have the least amount of faith because they are afraid of testing it." Part of being courageous means testing yourself, your beliefs, and the boundaries of your comfort zone.

It means taking the chance of being wrong or getting wounded because the growth, wisdom, and rewards earned (personal development, stronger relationships, financial abundance) are worth it.

Part of being courageous means testing yourself and your beliefs. It's taking the chance of being wrong because the potential rewards are worth it.

Expanding Your Comfort Zone

Have you ever thought, *I'm afraid to make a change because what if things get worse?* In 99% of the cases, that does not happen. Things only worsen when you don't do anything to improve your situation. One way to challenge being afraid of the unknown is to ponder the following: Would you go to the movies if you knew the ending of every single film? That wouldn't be much fun, right? Much of the enjoyment comes from not knowing what's going to happen. When going to the movies, aren't you also assuming it will be a pleasurable experience? Then why not think of your life as a movie that's full of possibility, and you have the directorial power to ensure it has a happy ending.

If you find yourself retreating to old excuses at any time, reassure yourself that you are in the process of developing courageous beliefs and habits. Your comfort zone will expand over time, and you will feel more secure, even in uncomfortable or uncertain situations. A few months from now when you look back upon this time, you'll feel proud of yourself. If it matters any, I'm proud of you for having the courage to take this impactful journey. You, my friend, are a pretty big deal.

Your Next Step

Add the "Empowering Statements" you wrote down underneath the "Comfort Zone Statements" earlier to your list of "Prosperity

Affirmations" in Chapter One or the space provided at the end of this book. Read them to yourself each day. Over time, these statements will become the fuel that increases the inner peace and abundant prosperity you'll be experiencing.

CHAPTER 5
MINDSET RESET

"Don't limit yourself! You can go as far as your mind lets you. What you believe, you can achieve."

Mary Kay Ash, Founder of Mary Kay Cosmetics

Up to this point, we've concentrated on unconscious beliefs. It's now time to upgrade your conscious thinking habits.

If you're going to utilize the full power of your mind to create your life by design, start by thinking about your goals in a pleasurable, positive, and inspiring way. In doing so, you accomplish two things. First, you'll provide your "inner genie" with the wishes you want it to grant. Second, what you say to yourself, and imagine in your mind, determines how you emotionally feel in the present moment. Those emotional states (feelings) dictate what actions you take, and those choices then move you toward the desired outcome.

Let's review this again. Your thoughts generate the feelings you experience. Those feelings determine what kind of choices you make. Those choices influence the results you get, and those results reinforce the thinking that started it all. It's a big circle. Your thoughts create your life.

Many think that one's quality of life is based upon the circumstances surrounding them, and I'd agree that your environment, religion, culture, and parenting had a tremendous influence. Yet, it does not mean you have zero control over your destiny. In this precise moment, it's not what you've experienced that controls you, but how you are presently interpreting what those experiences meant. Are you using your past as a justification to keep you from improving your situation, or are you using your history as an example of how not to live? It's not the experiences, but how you describe them to yourself, and the meaning you give to them puts everything else into motion.

Dr. Wayne Dyer once told the following story (I'm paraphrasing here, but this was his main idea): "I was taking a drive one day, and as I drove, I passed an affluent neighborhood, I saw homeowners cutting their grass, planting flowers, and keeping their homes looking nice. These are busy people, yet they made time to take care of their stuff because they appreciated it. A while later, I drove past a lower-income neighborhood and noticed the grass was tall, there was trash in the yard, and many of the homes were not well kept. Some might say it's because these homeowners didn't have the extra money, but it costs nothing to pick up the garbage and put it into the trashcan. *But they might be struggling with unemployment*. If that homeowner were unemployed, wouldn't they have lots of time to take care of their home or yard? It's a mindset. Your circumstances don't create you; they reveal your way of thinking." This coincides with the same findings of Earl Nightingale.

If your life is not the way you want it to be, change it. If you say, "Okay, let's do it," you'll begin the process of manifesting a higher quality of life. If your reaction is, "Yeah, right! Easier said than done. I can't do anything to change my situation," then you just set in motion a chain of events that will keep things the way they are.

The good news is that you have the power to move from surviving to thriving any time you wish. Right now, you can begin to create a new dialogue with yourself that is loving, supportive, hopeful, and encouraging. The grass isn't greener on the other side; it's greener wherever you water it.

"Mindset Reset" Experience

If your self-talk isn't supportive, encouraging, and focused on moving you toward a desirable outcome, use the following three-step process to improve it.

Step 1

Become more aware of your daily self-talk.

Pay attention to what you are saying to yourself all day. You have approximately 60,000 thoughts each day, and most of them are the same thoughts on repeat. If I followed you around and recorded your thoughts on any given day, what would most of them center on? Is the conversation you're having with yourself inspiring or scaring you? Is it supportive or skeptical? Are your comments encouraging or making you angry? Are you fixated on achieving a goal or obsessed with reasons for why you aren't making progress? You can't improve what you are not aware of. Step one is to pay attention to what you're saying, and imagining in your mind, each day.

What you think about comes about, so what are you thinking about?

Step 2

When a negative (fearful, unwanted, unkind) idea pops into your mind, immediately interrupt, challenge, and replace that thought with a more empowering (confident, desirable, kind) one.

You can interrupt the negative thought by imagining a big, red stop sign jumping up in the front of your mind. Then, say out loud three times like a magic spell, "CANCEL, CLEAR!" Make sure to say this out loud so you hear yourself taking charge. As you do this, the thought and accompanying feeling(s) will shrink and begin to fade. If it lingers, you'll need to challenge it.

You've already learned some effective strategies for challenging negative thoughts in previous chapters. You can repeat the self-defeating comment and then:

a) Yell, "What a bunch of BS!"

b) Run it through the Belief Upgrader.

c) Or, move the thought into the "false" folder.

You Can Also Do the Following

Often, you'll find yourself using words like "always" or "never" when being overly critical or dramatic. If you catch yourself using words like this, emphasize that word, challenge the statement, and replace it with more supportive affirmations.

For example, "Things never work out for me!" becomes "*Never?* Nothing has *ever* worked out for me, *ever?*" It forces you to bring the situation back into proportion. "Okay, lots of things have worked out for me; it's just that *this* hasn't happened yet. But it still can. I need to keep my eyes on the prize!"

Here's another example. "Why does this always happen to me?" becomes "Does it *always* happen to me? *Always?* No, not every time. It's happening *this* time, and I'm upset about it, but that's okay. I know I'm smart and resourceful, and I *will* find a way. This is a temporary situation, and I'm going to reach out to others who can help me get to my desired destination. I know things are going to turn out even better than I imagined. I've got this!"

These are examples of using positive self-talk to transform an upsetting situation into one where you feel more reassured and supported. Even if there is some truth to the negative commentary, own it, and improve the situation. Just making yourself feel bad is a waste of your brainpower. Some think beating up on themselves will somehow motivate them to improve things. Yet, bullying yourself only leads to discouragement and procrastination. Remember, your unconscious mind wants to avoid pain. If your primary motivational strategy is to scare or tear yourself down, your brain will trick you into avoiding situations that bring about these feelings.

Procrastination occurs when your mind associates pain or discomfort to specific behavior. Many people dislike exercising because of the false idea of "no pain, no gain." The secret to having lifelong motivation is to use positive reinforcement by intentionally associating pleasure to your goal, and the action steps that lead to it. Research has proven time and again that positive reinforcement is the most effective way to generate long-term commitments.

STEP 3

Replace un-useful (negative) thoughts with more useful, empowering affirmations.

It's essential to upgrade your thoughts rather than just ceasing to criticize yourself. Imagine your mind is like a mental flower garden. Your goal is to pull the weeds and plant more flowers. If you only focus on killing the weeds, the garden soil could become toxic, and the flowers won't grow either. Instead, spend more of your time watering the flowers so you end up with more of them. Too often, people are watering their mental weeds while simultaneously complaining about having so many of them. If you desire more roses in your garden, you'll need to plant "rose seeds." If you wish for your life to go in a specific direction, you must plant the corresponding mental seeds that will take you there!

Use these two questions to help clarify what mental seeds to plant in your mind:

1. Where would I like to be (or what would I love to accomplish) in thirty days, six months, one year, or three years?
2. What am I hoping to feel (what emotional states) as a result of accomplishing these goals?

Once you clarify the answers to these questions, begin planting those mental seeds by doing the following:

1. Imagine yourself already having what you desire so your inner genie knows what to manifest.
2. Spend most of your time thinking about what steps you can take today to bring about those outcomes. Become obsessed with the flowers, not the weeds.

Here are a few "prosperity seeds" for you to begin planting in your mind. Add these to your list of "Prosperity Affirmations" and repeat them out loud to yourself each morning and night.

Prosperity Affirmations (Seeds)

- Things do work out for me, and I'm always expecting new opportunities and blessings to show up each day.
- I learn from every experience, and this makes me stronger and wiser.
- There is no failure, only feedback.
- I am the person I was born to be, and every day in every way, I am getting better and better.
- My thoughts, feelings, values, and beliefs are just as important as anyone else's, and I am just as important as everyone else.

- I am powerful and possess the ability to make my dreams come true.
- Today is my day. I can never get it back, so I choose to get the most out of it.

Sometimes the easiest way to come up with a more empowering belief is to say the opposite of the negative sentiment. "I can't do it" becomes "I can do it!" "I'm not worthy" becomes "I am worthy!" "It will never happen" becomes "It's happening!"

Too often, people are watering their mental weeds while simultaneously complaining about having so many of them!

You Become What You Repeat

People often describe themselves as a positive thinker or a negative thinker. Yet, I prefer to substitute the word "positive" with "useful" and "proactive" and the word "negative" with "destructive" and "hurtful" thinking. These words better describe the outcomes produced by your self-talk (the conversations you have with yourself all day long). We are not born as positive or negative human beings. Sure, you may be more of a solution-finder or problem-solver, yet it's how you practice directing your thoughts that determine the quality of your life.

When those who struggle with low self-esteem or attain their goals are asked to practice using proactive self-talk for two weeks, many give up by the first day. Clients have told me, "That positive thinking stuff doesn't work. I'm just fooling (or lying to) myself." I typically reply, "You're right. You are fooling yourself if you think proactive thinking doesn't work. How long did you practice it?" The answer I hear most is, "Well, I got busy with other things." Translated, that means they didn't practice at all.

If you hear something enough, eventually you start believing it. People buy into negative opinions about themselves only because those ideas have been reinforced far more times than any positive remarks.

Sometimes I'm asked, "How long do I need to do this positive thinking stuff?" The answer is: As long as it takes for it to become natural because there is nothing of greater importance than understanding how to influence your thinking. My grandfather taught me the value of doing things right and persisting until I succeeded.

I recall being fifteen years old and struggling to figure something out. I finally got so frustrated that I yelled, "How many times do I have to do this?" He replied, "Until you get it right." Shortly after that, I did figure it out. I wasn't happy with my grandfather's answer, but when I finally accomplished the goal, it was the best feeling ever. If I had it my way, I would have quit far before I ever got to experience the joyful feeling of success. Thank goodness I had someone who could see beyond my frustrations and show me the bigger picture. I hope my words are doing this for you right now.

You can accomplish more than you've ever imagined if you continue to push past your self-doubt or desire to give in.

If you want to believe something better about yourself, say something better to yourself so often that you can't recall anything else. If you could free yourself from emotional pain and significantly elevate your quality of life, but the catch is you have to repeat specific prosperity affirmations to yourself ten thousand times in a row for it to happen, would you do it? If so, today is the perfect day to get started.

People buy into negative opinions about themselves because those ideas have been reinforced far more times than any positive remarks.

Tony Robbins said, "Repetition is the mother of all skill." Many of the things you now do with ease were once difficult tasks you had to practice and repeat, such as speaking, writing, tying your shoes, driving a car, beginning a new job, etc. When my son first started walking, he fell a lot. Do you think he was telling himself, *This is a dumb idea; I'm never going to walk! Why does this keep happening to me?* No, that's ridiculous. He got up and tried again and again until he succeeded. Why? Because he was determined to accomplish his goal, and he wasn't going to let anything stop him. By the way, didn't you have the same attitude? After all, you learned to walk too, right? Once you begin to think success, your odds of succeeding increase dramatically.

"Mindset Reset" Review

Step 1

Become more aware of your daily self-talk.

Step 2

When a negative (fearful, unwanted, unkind) idea pops into your mind, immediately interrupt, challenge, and replace the thought with a more empowering (confident, desirable, kind) one.

Step 3

Replace un-useful (negative) thoughts with more useful, empowering affirmations.

Over time, the following three steps will become automatic (a habit). You'll still need to monitor your thoughts each day to ensure you're staying on course, but the mindfulness will eventually become second nature.

The grass isn't greener on the other side. It's greener wherever you water it!

CHAPTER 6

BELIEVING IN YOU

"I've missed more than 9,000 shots in my career. I've lost almost 300 games. Twenty-six times I've been trusted to take the game-winning shot and missed. I've failed over and over and over again in my life, and that is why I succeed."

Michael Jordan, NBA legendary basketball MVP

I've had the privilege of coaching thousands of people who feared they'd never accomplish their goals—and then they did. Arlene came to see me for weight loss. She had not lost a single pound in over twenty years and blamed it on her arthritis and having a bad thyroid. Through our coaching sessions, Arlene shared that most of her day was spent sitting because of her health challenges. Even though she wasn't eating that poorly, there was no physical exercise in her routine. I encouraged Arlene to start moving more to strengthen her body and spirit. That's when the self-limiting beliefs emerged. "I'm too old to exercise. I could get hurt. My physical problems are what's keeping me heavy."

Two weeks later, I facilitated a group class that taught how to triumph over self-sabotaging beliefs and invited Arlene to attend. We went through a couple of experiences in this book and ended the course with a board-breaking ceremony. Each person wrote down their worries and fears on a wooden board. Then they handed me the board, held it, and broke it in two with the palm of their hand like a karate master.

Arlene nervously stepped up and handed me her board. She said, "I'm seventy-two years old, and I have arthritis in my hands." I smiled and said, "Arlene, the board doesn't exist. I want you to move your hand to the imaginary target behind this board just like I taught you."

When breaking boards, you don't focus on hitting the board. You imagine hitting a target on the other side of it. The same holds true for achieving goals. Don't focus on the obstacles in front of you. Instead, aim for the desired outcome on the other side of the barrier. Arlene took a deep breath, aimed at her target, and thrust her hand forward. The board snapped in two like a twig. Arlene looked at the two pieces of broken board and then at her palm in disbelief. I passed her the broken board and said, "So much for being too old." She smiled broadly, and the whole class cheered. Two months later, Arlene was down fifteen pounds!

Don't focus on the obstacles in front of you. Instead, aim for the desired outcome on the other side of the barrier.

The inner critic is the voice in your mind warning you to be cautious, suspicious, or fearful. These thoughts can have value at times, especially in situations where you should be careful. Yet, most of what comes from your inner critic is not useful. Jane, a client, once said she was no longer going to tolerate her own "stinking thinking." She exclaimed, "You know what? I'm tired of constantly bullying myself. It's exhausting, and I'm sick of hurting my own feelings all the time." Jane decided to believe more in herself and her abilities that day, and that decision made all the difference. You can make the same decision today. Make comments to yourself that leave you feeling empowered and strong. If you don't believe the new things you are saying at first, that's okay. Anything new doesn't feel comfortable or familiar at first. But over time, it will.

One of the most important keys to experiencing an extraordinary life is to learn how to communicate more encouragingly with yourself.

Ask "Power" Questions

The process of thinking mostly consists of asking and answering questions in your mind. "Am I hungry? What should I eat? What sounds good? How about a burger? No, I had that yesterday. What about a salad? Okay. Should I try that new dressing?" You are continually having conversations with yourself, whether by literally speaking to yourself or running pictures or movies in your mind. These words and images directly influence how you feel and the actions you take every minute of the day. You never *just* feel an emotion. There is always something that you picture or say to yourself that precedes the emotional state, even if you aren't aware of it.

Your questions directly influence the quality of your life. If you ask yourself an empowering question, your brain will respond with an empowering answer. If you ask a fear-based question, your mind will provide you with a fearful response. What you put in comes out. The more solution-oriented your internal questions are, the more your brain will provide methods for moving you to your desired destination.

"Fear-Based" Questions

- What's wrong with me?
- Why doesn't anything ever work out?

- What else could go wrong?
- Why me?
- Why this?
- Why now?
- Why can't I get what I want?
- Why does this always happen to me?
- What did I do to deserve this?
- Whose fault is this?
- Why does the world hate me?
- Why do I always sabotage myself?
- Why do people treat me this way?
- Why is the world so evil?
- Why are people so untrustworthy?
- Will I always be broke (or broken)?

"Why" questions often point you in the wrong direction. They fixate your attention on the pole or weed (problem) instead of on the solution (stay on the road/flowers). Instead, begin using proactive questions, or what I refer to as "Power" questions. They typically start with the words "what" or "how."

As in, "What am I going to do about it?" or "How can I make this activity more enjoyable?"

"Power Questions" Experience

The questions you ask yourself influence the way you feel and behave. Use this four-step "Power Question" Experience to move from surviving to thriving.

STEP 1

Think of something that is a problem in your life right now. Write it below.

Current Problem:

____

____

____

STEP 2

As you think about this problem, ask yourself the following fear-based questions out loud. Don't bother answering the questions. Just notice how asking them makes you feel.

Why do I have this problem?
How long have I had it?
How does this limit me?
How does this problem prevent me from doing what I want?
Whose fault is it that I have this problem?
What bad things could happen in the future because I have this problem?

How are you feeling right now? Do you feel sad, frustrated, scared, or mad? It's not because of the situation but as a result of asking those lousy questions! These are the common questions people ask themselves when feeling stressed or stuck, leading to self-pity, anger, blame, and helplessness. Instead of focusing on how to get past your obstacles, fear-based questions focus you on the challenges themselves, which causes them to appear larger than they are. Let's try something different.

STEP 3

Think about the problem you wrote down in step one and then ask yourself the following questions out loud. Notice if you feel any different asking yourself these questions, as opposed to the lousy ones.

What outcome do I want?
Why do I want this?
How will it feel when I've accomplished this goal?
How will I know that I've reached my destination?
When I get what I want, what else in my life will improve?
Who can I reach out to for help with this?
What resources do I need to get to the next step/level?
How can I best utilize the resources I already have?
How would I like to feel right now?
What's one thing I can do to start feeling this way?

Feel any different now? Instead of concentrating on what's wrong or conjuring up future worst-case scenarios, "Power" questions help you realize what's within your control. They also subconsciously reinforce the assumption that you *will* attain your goal. Asking high-caliber questions helps you feel hopeful, capable, and motivated for action.

STEP 4

In the space below, write down the problem you started with from Step 1.

Current Challenge (problem)

____

____

Next, jot down the Power Questions you want to start asking to solve issues like this now and in the future.

1.

2.

3.

4.

5.

6.

7.

Finally, take a few minutes to answer those questions below. You'll have a clear plan for how to effectively address and solve this issue.

1.

2.

3.

4.

5.

6.

7.

Asking proactive questions will cause your brain to respond with action steps that will begin producing positive results when immediately acted upon.

When you readjust your mental focus by asking "Power" questions, you leap past the inner critic and enter a more resourceful state of mind. In this state, you will discover the options that evaded your conscious awareness in the past. Operating at a higher level of consciousness (awareness) allows you to identify action steps that produce the desired outcomes in the shortest amount of time.

"Quality questions create a quality life. Successful people ask better questions, and as a result, they get better answers."
Anthony Robbins

CHAPTER 7
YOUR AWAKENING

"You are an oak tree! Stop thinking like the acorn you originated from."
Jim Cathcart, CSP, author of *The Acorn Principle*

The importance of uncovering and upgrading unconscious beliefs that hold you back from reaching your full potential has been established. Now it's time to facilitate your awakening.

After facilitating tens of thousands of individual sessions helping people triumph over every possible trauma and challenge, one primal fear stimulates all the rest. "I'm not (good) enough. Therefore, I won't be loved."

This fear develops at an early age and causes your brain to build coping (survival) strategies to get love, attention, or approval. The question then becomes, "What do I need to do, or who do I need to be, to survive or receive love?"

A considerable part of my life was spent chasing the approval of others. In my early twenties, I began to keep a journal. Those pages were filled with thoughts and feelings of hurt, anger, frustration, and self-pity. I didn't like myself much at the time, mostly because of all the poor choices I made trying to get people to like me.

I'd hurt my friend's feelings just to get a laugh from a group of strangers or run up credit card debt buying people dinner even though I was broke. My relationships were fueled with insecurity. My desperation and fear that others would abandon me caused me to be so jealous that it tore apart relationships and produced the very consequences I feared. At the time, I thought all these heart-wrenching things were happening *to* me, rather than taking ownership of the fact that I was causing most of my problems.

Around the age of twenty-two, I moved out of my dad's house into this old, beat-up apartment owned by a Polish church. The rent was $150 a month, and I remember worrying all the time about how I was going to cover it. One day, I was sitting out back on the steps gazing over the parking lot. I was having another bad day as an avalanche of hurtful memories from the past poured through my mind.

I didn't know how to resolve hurts from the past, so I continually recycled them in my mind. The more fear, anger, resentment, and self-pity I held, the more my mind was bombarded with past images that generated those emotions. Yet, on this day, something completely unexpected occurred.

I was reviewing a painful memory from my past, and a new thought popped into my mind: *Why don't you change the memory?* I reacted by thinking, *Can you do that?* The response I got back from my subconscious was, *It's your imagination. You can do whatever you want with it.* So I figured I'd try it out on a hurtful memory from when I was sixteen years old.

I met a girl who was visiting her dad down the street from where I grew up. She made my heart race, and it took me a long time to muster up the nerve to ask her to go for a walk with me that afternoon. It would be my first official date, and I was flying high as a kite when she said yes.

Finally, the hour had arrived, so I quickly walked down the street to her dad's house and knocked on the door. It opened, and she looked at me a bit puzzled. "What are you doing here?" Confused, I said, "I'm here to pick you up. We are hanging out, right?" She replied, "I thought you weren't feeling well today." I returned her puzzled look.

She continued, "Chris told me you were sick and that he'd keep me company until you felt better." Chris was my childhood best friend. I felt sick to my stomach at the thought of him purposefully betraying me, but that wasn't the worst part. I told her what he had done, but she decided to go hang out with him anyway. I felt crushed twice in the same five minutes by two people I cared about most.

As I sat on the steps remembering the betrayal of 1986, the same rush of anger and hurt rushed through my body as it did back then. Then I had the idea again. *Why don't you change the memory? After all, they are* your *memories. You can do whatever you want with them.*

I was in the fourth year of college, working toward a degree in clinical psychology. During one of my classes, we were taught that the past's recollected accounts were not perfectly captured experiences. In fact, much of what people remembered from the past wasn't as accurate as they thought. Plus, the more time that had passed, the lower the accuracy of recalling what actually occurred.

If your brain doesn't capture all the precise details of a situation, it makes things up to fill in the blanks. This is done out of your conscious awareness. It's called confabulation. The only reason the brain stores memory in the first place is to learn from past experiences to avoid danger in the present. As I think about that memory over thirty years later, I doubt that I told the girl what Chris had done. Instead, I probably just looked at her and walked away. Telling her what had happened would have been much too mature for me at the time.

The details that construct one's memories are not as crucial to your brain as interpreting what that information means. Your subjective analysis of a situation is more powerful than the experience itself. It's not what you go through, but what your brain thinks it means. Your mind's unconscious translation about a situation you experience becomes a belief, and those expectations rule over your destiny.

If you're a small child and see a mouse, your brain might think, *That fuzzy animal is cute,* and the belief that you like animals is formed. If you see that mouse, and then watch your mother scream and jump up on a chair, your brain might form a belief that small animals are dangerous. It's not the mouse itself, but whether your mind decides the mouse is safe or hazardous that influences you most.

We can't change the past, but you can update the resulting beliefs. You can also use your imagination to "edit" memories in a way that empowers you. When viewpoints are modified, your feelings and behaviors transform as well.

I wondered what would happen if I imagined traveling back in time and handling the situation differently with Chris and the girl who broke my heart. I began conjuring up new scenarios where I confronted my best friend and had him apologize to me. Then, instead of feeling weak and insignificant, I took a stand for myself. I imagined informing the girl that if she was dumb enough to go out with Chris after hearing what had happened, I didn't want anything to do with her. I then imagined her apologizing as well. Again, instead of feeling helpless, I took my power back.

Suddenly, I started feeling a little better. I sat up taller and felt more empowered. This was surprising because I was just making this stuff up in my imagination. But isn't that what we always do? When you worry about the future, aren't you creating worst-case scenarios in your head that haven't happened and then emotionally reacting as if they had? As I discovered that day, it doesn't matter what really happened. All that matters is the meaning you decide to give it.

When I envisioned these kids apologizing to me, I began to feel better. It wasn't happening for real, but in my mind, it felt good anyway, and that's the point. You may have been hurt or wronged by someone who will never apologize. They might even be deceased. But it doesn't matter because your emotional freedom is not dependent on the actions of someone else. You have the power to set yourself free.

When I started visualizing getting what I wanted or needed, I felt more in control and peaceful inside. It did not require somebody else to say or do something for me to feel better. I had the power to make myself feel happier, and that was a massive revelation.

A few years later, I began taking others back through time to reclaim their power. People started giving themselves the love, acceptance, support, encouragement, and protection they needed, rather than waiting for someone else to rescue them. I used to think the love and safety we crave are supposed to be satisfied by those around us. After twenty-five years of taking people through this awakening experience, it's clear the one you need the most love and approval from is yourself.

I watched thousands of people's lives dramatically improve from going through this one experience alone. It didn't matter what they had come in for; this experience shifted them in a beautifully sustainable way. Trauma survivors healed, those who couldn't lose weight did, and people with a wide variety of phobias, bad habits, and physical pains got better.

I started calling this process the "Awakening" Experience because it awakens your true potential. You don't need anyone's permission to feel loved, safe, or affirmed. You can give this to yourself right now. If you don't believe it or feel worthy of feeling good, it's only because of how you are interpreting your past and what you think it means about you.

I used to believe I had to be rich or famous to feel worthwhile. I was neither, so did that mean I was doomed to feel "less than" forever? At the time, I thought so. I would think to myself, *I'll be happy when I have more money, I'm in a happier relationship, drive a fancy car, and being admired by millions.* But this was all a trap.

In the old black-and-white movies, there was a famous performer named Charlie Chaplin. In one of his classic routines, his derby hat would fall onto the floor. As he stooped to pick it up, he'd simultaneously kick the derby hat out of reach with his foot. He'd then strut over to the hat, lean over to snatch it up, and then kick it out of reach. Charlie would do this repeatedly, shuffling around the room, attempting to pick up the hat that was always just out of reach.

Charlie's hat represents happiness and inner peace. Most of us are going through life, kicking the hat away from our grasp without realizing it. Of course, this isn't always the case. Often, things happen that are out of your control. Yet, it's not what shows up, but how you show up that ultimately determines your quality of life.

Your emotional freedom is not dependent on the actions of someone else. You have the power to set yourself free.

THE "AWAKENING" EXPERIENCE

As you move through this experience, I strongly recommended reading through the entire description of this journey. Then, go through it again and do what is described. This can be an intensely emotional experience. You'll want to know what to do before going through each part of the journey. If you feel it would be better to have someone guide you through this experience, please contact my office, and we'll arrange an appointment after reading through the description. You can also visit www.surviv-ingtothriving.me/awakening

While going through this mental exercise, it won't matter whether you picture the scenarios in your imagination, or just talk yourself through them. Do whatever makes you feel more comfortable.

Begin by taking slow breaths in through your nose, down to the bottom of your lungs, and then slowly exhale. Focus on the cool air coming into your body, and the warm air leaving. Pretend the fresh air is healing oxygen that flows down into the center of your body, making everything feel open, bright, and safe inside.

Every time you exhale, imagine stress leaving the body in the form of warm air. Scoop up the tension, breathe it out, and send it away. Take a few moments and do this now.

Next, bring warm sunshine from a bright summer's day into the room and imagine pouring that soothing sunshine down over you. Allow that healing light to cascade down through your scalp, relaxing your head, neck, and shoulders. As the warm sunshine massages across your shoulder blades, it then flows down your spine, allowing the larger muscles and the smaller ones to soften, loosen, and let go.

As you continue breathing in through your nose, imagine sending that sunshine down to your toes. Feel the relaxation moving through your legs, as all remaining pressure flows out through the soles of your feet. Take a few moments to imagine this now.

Allow this light to shine so brightly, it surrounds you in a beautiful field of protective light. This glowing light locks in all the peaceful feelings flowing within you, while blocking out any negative energy. You'll be surrounded in this protective force field of energy throughout the rest of this journey.

As your body continues to relax, we will begin the process of upgrading any self-limiting beliefs that are holding you back from your greatness. To find the belief, we start with conjuring the uncomfortable feeling that's linked to it.

Once you connect with that feeling, you will be instructed to follow this feeling back to the first time you remember feeling that emotion. As you imagine traveling back in time, you're not going to relive anything. Instead, you'll imagine whatever comes to mind as though it's happening in a movie, on a television, located on the other side of the room. You'll also be holding a magic remote control that can stop, fast-forward, pause, mute, and turn off this movie whenever you wish. You are in complete control/

When you are ready, begin connecting with the feeling that arises whenever you feel blocked, anxious, angry, resentful, or scared. Allow it to bubble up to the surface and notice where you feel the sensation. Is it in your head, chest, stomach, or somewhere else? As you start to connect with this emotion, imagine stepping into it and following the feeling back to the event or situation that's most responsible for it.

You can also close your eyes and count from three down to one as you follow the feeling back to the first time you recall feeling that specific emotion. Once a memory has emerged, open your eyes, and continue reading.

Notice whatever comes to mind. Are you inside or outside? Are you alone or with someone? How old are you in this memory? As you observe the memory unfold on the television across the room, notice what your younger self is experiencing. If anything upsetting, scary, or dangerous comes up, immediately pause the memory with your magic remote control. You can then imagine sending your protective light around the younger version of you so they are now safe. If other people were involved in that situation, imagine them fading away. The younger version of you is now safe and secure.

Think about how much you've learned about life since you were this age, and how the wisdom gained would have benefitted you back then. Now you have an opportunity to love, protect, and empower this younger version of you. At your current age, and with the wisdom you've learned, imagine floating back through time into that situation with your younger self.

Your younger self is surprised to see you, but also relieved. Ask them what they need most from you. Do they need more love, acceptance, support, encouragement, or protection? Maybe they need all of it, or something else. Ask this younger version what they need most from you and then listen for the response.

Whatever this younger child has asked for, it's time for you to provide it. Often, the request is to be loved, accepted, and encouraged more by you. Your inner child wants to feel safe and be reassured that everything is going to be okay. Whatever this younger version of you said they needed, give it to them now.

If you found a lost and scared child, would you tell her to shut up because things are never going to be better for her? No, because that would be cruel. It's time to direct this compassion inward. If the younger you asked for more love, love them. Put your arm around them and offer a big hug. Then say, "I'm here for you now, and I am going to love, support, protect, and encourage you for the rest of your life."

Then say, "You were born a perfect creation from the universe. You are already more than enough. You are already good and don't have to prove anything. You are already enough, and I love you."

If this part of you desires more self-acceptance, provide it. If they are afraid of being abandoned, let them know, "I'm going to always be here for you from now on. I'm going to take care of you the way you deserve to be cared for, and you'll never be alone because I'll always be by your side."

If what's needed is understanding or support, provide it through someone who has greater wisdom or clarity of why others may have behaved so immaturely. See others in your life as fellow wounded children who acted out or coped in the only way they knew how. Bring compassion into the room, first for yourself, and then for others.

If they need to feel safer, imagine surrounding them in the same protective light that shines around you. Shrink the details of the memory while having the younger you feel one hundred feet tall. Then show them how to breathe through the nose, down to the belly, and then slowly exhale to increase feelings of confidence and peace.

If what's desired is encouragement, you can provide that as well. If you're not exactly sure what to say, think about what you might say to a friend or child you care about. What would you say to that person to help them feel safe or encouraged? When more encouraging remarks come to mind, relay them to the younger version of you. Or, think of what you wished someone would have told you, that would have set you emotionally free, and say that to your inner child.

Ask yourself the right questions, and the answers will appear. When they do, say those words to your younger self and set yourself free. Take as much time as you need, and do this now.

Now imagine yourself confident, empowered, and standing tall, with your shoulders back, and a smile on your face. It's wonderful. The final step is to upgrade the outdated belief. Remember, it's not what you experience, but the interpretation of what it means that matters most. Therefore, I want you to ask this younger version of you what the old, fearful belief was that you used to have due to that situation.

Once you've identified what the fearful, self-limiting belief was, then ask the more important question: "What would you rather believe about yourself instead? If you can believe anything you want, what would you rather believe instead that would help you feel more empowered for the rest of your life?"

Once you have identified the updated belief, turn it into an "I am" statement. "I am (good) enough. I am worthy. I am loved. I am safe. I can trust myself. I am beautiful. I am free." I am !"

Imagine giving this younger version of you one more hug, and as they hug you back, imagine hearing them whisper, "Thank you" in your ear. Then they melt into your body and are absorbed into your heart, where they will now live. Then, take your younger self out of that old situation because you no longer need it. That memory can fade away now because you've collected the wisdom learned from it. Then float back up through the years to the present moment with your new empowered belief firmly in place.

Now that you have reclaimed your power from the past, it's time to briefly visit the future. Imagine yourself floating into the near future and notice how much more enjoyable your life has become with this new belief guiding your life. You are safe, loved, and more than enough. Fancy yourself looking the way you want to, feeling the way you want to, and behaving in ways that leave you feeling proud of yourself.

There's a new sense of confidence and worthiness that shines brightly inside of you. It gives you the ability to take action, reach for what you want, and actually get it. Your inner light shines so brightly, it causes the entire universe to take notice. Because the world is like a mirror, reflecting back whatever you send out, you now find more light, love, and opportunities flooding into your life. It's thrilling, and you love how good it feels. Take this feeling and absorb it into every cell of your body Spend a few moments enjoying the future you have created for yourself, and the happiness that comes with it.

When you've locked those images and feelings in your mind, return to the present moment. Finally, tell yourself that when you count to five and open your eyes, a new chapter will begin, and it's a good one. Then, slowly count from one up to five, feeling an immense sense of pride for having the courage to go down this rarely traveled path. When you reach number five, take one more breath in through your nose and slowly open your eyes.

Now that you've read the instructions, return to the start of "Your Awakening" and go through the exercise. Take your time and do this now. It's worth it—and so are you.

RECAP

This experience can transform your life, but it's just one of the steps in the journey. If you had difficulty with any part of it, I encourage you to have someone trained to take people through this experience to guide you through it. If you'd like me to take you through it, I have a recorded session available here at www.survivingtothriving.me/awakening

People often ask if they can go through other situations from the past and reclaim their power using this exercise. The answer is yes. Now that you know how to reframe your memories and upgrade beliefs, you can use this tool as many times as you'd like. If, for example, you recall being humiliated by a teacher in front of the class, and it created a fear of public speaking, you can revisit that moment and create an "awakening."

Imagine helping that younger version of you feel safe, empowered, and confident standing in front of your peers. Have your teacher apologize for (intentionally or unintentionally) hurting your feelings, and imagine your classmates giving you a standing ovation. Then upgrade the belief from "I can't speak in front of others" to "I can speak confidently in front of others, and I'm going to invest in my ability to do so."

Upgrading your beliefs will give you the courage to invest in your abilities. If you want to feel safer, your new vision of yourself will fuel the motivation to participate in strength training or self-defense classes. If you believe that you can be a confident public speaker or anything else, invest in education that leads to that outcome.

As you continue realizing how powerful your imagination is, you'll find more ways of using it to your advantage. You can break the spells of your past and take control of your present. Then I'll show you how to create your future.

CHAPTER 8
THE PATH TO INNER PEACE

"Change the changeable, accept the unchangeable, and remove yourself from the unacceptable."

Dr. Denis Waitley, author of *The Psychology of Winning*

Now that you have experienced an awakening, it's time to free yourself from blocked energy that may be clogging your ability to manifest whatever your heart desires. We'll initiate the Power of Forgiveness to release you from the negative energy that binds you to your past. Forgiveness is frequently misunderstood, which is why it's not used as regularly as it should be.

When you forgive someone, it does not mean that what you've experienced was okay. It does not mean others are somehow off the hook, or that you must forget about what occurred. Often, we are afraid to forgive and forget because that means it could happen again. We use our anger and hurt as protection. Yet walking around with your guard up only attracts more of what you fear. Plus, the wall you put up to protect yourself from others has also now made you a prisoner inside it. That wall is no longer keeping you from experiencing pain; it's become the reason why you're still in it.

When you forgive someone, it releases you from the negative energy and painful memories of your past. When I imagined forgiving my best friend for "stealing my girl" when I was sixteen, I felt a sense of peace wash over me. Yes, that memory did happen, and I wouldn't want it to occur again. Yet, when I forgave, it set me free, and its remembrance stopped coming up. It was there for me to learn forgiveness. Once I got the message, the messenger was no longer needed.

If you are holding a grudge, you're the one holding it. Buddha once said that holding resentment is like drinking poison and expecting someone else to die. Forgiveness releases a kind of inner freedom within you. It reinforces the fact that your human spirit is more powerful than any experience you may have. You are connected to a fantastic universe with unlimited possibilities. You contain the same potential as the wisest beings that have ever roamed this planet.

Jesus said to love your enemies, not because he was afraid, but because he knew that love and forgiveness were the most enormous forces in the universe. You can choose to forgive people as Buddha did, create peace like Nelson Mandela, or love like Jesus. You have this ability. Whether you use it or not is a choice that will shape your destiny.

I recently took a client through the "Forgiveness" Experience you are about to encounter. Afterward, she said, "I just realized that even though I love my husband, children, and friends, there was always a thread of resentment that's kept me from giving 100% of my love. As a child, it never felt like I got the attention I desired. When others did get that attention, even my kids, I subconsciously resented them. Yet, when forgiving my mother during this exercise, I realized she raised five of us because my dad was always at work. Now that I've forgiven her and myself for being so resentful, I feel a sense of peace inside. It's like I can give all of my love now. It's funny because I came here for something else and now, I don't even care about that. I feel so good inside." When you release hidden emotional blocks, the peace you feel is often immediate, and goals are easier to attain.

"FORGIVENESS" EXPERIENCE

We will approach this part of the journey in the same way you did with the "Awakening" Experience. Read through all the directions first then come back and reread the instructions as you imagine everything playing out in your mind.

Get into a comfortable position in a quiet place where you are alone and free to experience whatever emotions arise. Take a few slow breaths in through your nose, down to your belly, and slowly exhale.

Then imagine sunshine pouring down over the top of your head and moving down your body, relaxing each muscle along the way. Allow the muscles in your neck and shoulders to soften and loosen as the sunshine massages your arms, hands, and fingers.

Now move that sunshine through your lower body—all the way down to your toes. Allow any remaining tension to drain out through the soles of your feet.

The sunshine beams so brightly that it wraps you in a protective force field of light. Peacefully, you are then transported to a beautiful forest. Find yourself standing on a wooded path in this safe, calming place. Up ahead, you see a log cabin. Move toward this cabin, and upon reaching it, open the door and step inside. Once inside, you notice it's one giant room. Everything is white—the walls, floor, and ceiling. It's bright and feels safe.

The other unusual thing about this room is that it's divided in half by a massive glass piece. Although the glass is transparent, you cannot get to the other side of this room. Even if you hit the glass with a sledgehammer, it wouldn't scratch it. There's also a chair on the other side of the glass. In a moment, you're going to invite somebody into this room that you have held anger or resentment toward. You may know who to bring into the room, or it may surprise you who walks in.

When this person enters the room, they will immediately proceed to the chair on the opposite side of the glass from you and sit down. In the chair, they cannot talk, move, or make any facial expressions. What they *can* do is genuinely listen to what you have to say. This is a safe place, and you are in charge. When you are ready, have this person enter the room and sit in that chair.

You now have a powerful opportunity to get off your chest all the things you've ever wanted to say. You can cry, yell, swear, or calmly share whatever you need to say, so the anger or hurt can be released. You can do this in your mind or out loud. Take this moment to share whatever you feel needs to be expressed to free this blocked energy. All this person can do is genuinely listen. Take as much time you need, and when you're done, continue reading. Do this now.

Well done! Now, listen carefully. This person will respond to what you just said in the way you most want them to. They will express whatever it is you most need to hear so you can be free from the negative energy that keeps you stuck in the past. There may be an apology, explanation, or plea for forgiveness. They might also say things you wished would have been expressed back then. Whatever it is you need to hear to move forward, imagine receiving this now. When this is done, continue reading.

Excellent! Since you are in charge, you have the final word. You can respond to whatever was said or share anything else that comes to mind. When you have communicated whatever else needs to be said, continue reading.

Well done! The most important part of this experience is forgiveness. When forgiving another or oneself, it frees you from the negativity that keeps one stuck and unhappy. When this toxic energy is released, it can be replaced with inner peace, love, freedom, and prosperity. When you are ready to forgive this person, and free yourself, continue reading.

Excellent! When delaying forgiveness, it only prolongs your ability to move forward prosperously in life. Assuming you are ready to forgive, imagine an energy cord connected to you with the other end connected to the person on the other side of the glass. In a moment, you are going to say out loud five times in a row, "I forgive you, and I release you!" On the fifth time of saying, "I forgive you, and I release you!" imagine cutting the cord. You can karate chop it, use a lightsaber, or disconnect the cord in any other way you see fit. Do this now.

As you cut the energy cord in two, it dries up and detaches from you and the other person. The cord disintegrates into thin air while a rush of emotion pours out of your body. Gradually, you begin feeling lighter and more at ease.

You no longer need the other person in the room. Thus, you can have this person fade away. Or, you may decide to let the wall come down and offer a handshake or hug. Whatever you are most comfortable with. Do this now and then continue reading.

Leave this building and return to the wooded path. Notice it veers off to the left. Follow it and find yourself coming to an opening where a beautiful lake is revealed. Next to the lake on the shore, there's a magnificent bonfire. Sitting by the edge of the fire is a large box with a lid that's open. Approach the box and imagine removing any remaining negative energy left over from the events you recalled and place it into the box. You might visualize pulling a blob of dark energy out of your body or sending the last bit of tension through your fingertips, and placing it into the box. Then close the lid and lock it.

Pick the box up and heave it onto the bonfire. The fire represents cleansing, as it transforms the negative energy into neutral energy once more. Watch the flames dance up into the sky as the box and everything in it disintegrates. Stroll over to the water's edge and notice a beautiful twinkle of light coming down from the heavens. Sometimes, when we go through a traumatic event, it can feel like losing a piece of our innocence. However, it has found its way back home to you. As this sparkling light approaches, it seems to shine even brighter. It then flows right into you and is absorbed through your heart, as all the tiny pieces are now reassembled and more durable than ever.

Remember that it's not the experience itself. It's the belief(s) generated from it that determines how you think, feel, and behave. What was the outdated belief you used to have because of those memories?

Now, what would you like to believe about yourself instead, moving forward? You can adopt any more empowering viewpoint you wish. Thus, what new belief would strengthen you? Take as much time as you need with this, and then continue reading.

With your new belief and this feeling of peace within, imagine lifting into the sky, through the clouds, and then descending back down into the room where you began. Take a slow power breath in and think about your future with this new belief in place. Imagine yourself looking the way you want to look, feeling the emotions you've always desired, and making choices that leave you feeling proud of yourself afterward. When you've completed this, take one more slow power breath in and then write your new empowering belief below. Nice job!

New, Empowering Belief

"I   ."

FORGIVING YOURSELF

You now have a powerful strategy for releasing blocked energy that can be utilized as often as needed. There may be several people in your life you want to take into that room and forgive. It doesn't mean you need to have a relationship with any of these people. They never have to know you've done this exercise with them in mind. You can also bring those who have passed away into this healing place because your imagination has no boundaries. Remember, this experience has less to do with others in your past, and more to do with realizing you can set yourself free. You don't have to rely on anyone else to do the right thing.

Over the years, I've led thousands of people through this experience. On numerous occasions, people have said the person they needed to put in the chair on the other side of the glass was themselves. They had been blaming, shaming, or resenting themselves for way too long. This experience emphasizes that you can give yourself what you need, and that also means forgiving yourself for mistakes you've made. Sometimes, we only need to forgive ourselves for holding onto the grudges for so long.

Hindsight is 20/20. It's easy to look back and see where we might've gone wrong. Quit beating yourself up because it doesn't do anything to move you forward in a healthy way. It's not fair. Whatever choice or decision you made, you were doing the best you could then. Even if you knew you were behaving poorly at that moment, there were reasons why you were making those choices. Remember, your unconscious beliefs drive your behavior, and the unconscious mind doesn't care about right or wrong. It's concerned only with survival, and sometimes we make bad decisions as a result.

You may have experienced some form of mental, emotional, physical, or sexual abuse. In this case, it wasn't your fault at all. You were victimized, but that doesn't mean you have to be a lifelong victim. Why do bad things happen? Look at the world's state and all the brokenness in it, and you'll have the answer. Yet, I think it's the wrong question to dwell on. Some say we attract everything in our life. Others suggest our purpose is to grow spiritually, and we can only do this by experiencing adversity, injustice, and pain. If there were no problems or anxiety, there would be no point in growing.

The more important question is, "What am I going to do with this experience? Am I going to label myself a victim or victor? Am I going to survive, or use the energy from this experience to thrive?" Long ago, I decided to channel my pain and anxiety into helping others. As a result, my coaching programs have empowered tens of thousands of people. If I hadn't gone through those upsetting situations in the past, you wouldn't be reading this book. My painful past was necessary, but it no longer controls my feelings in the present, and I'm consciously co-creating my future with God.

Growing up in Indiana, I've gained a lot of "Farmer Wisdom." Farmers will tell you things grow better in manure. Thus, I chose to take the crap from my past and use it to grow my future. You can do the same. If you go through the "Forgiveness" Experience to forgive yourself, be extra compassionate to that younger you. They deserve all the love and kindness you can provide.

Need Help?

If you're having difficulty forgiving, get assistance with this. Having someone else provide feedback or sharing different points of view can be the secret to unlocking your inner freedom. If you'd like me to lead you through this, visit www.survivingto-thriving.me/releasing

CHAPTER 9
CLEARING BLOCKS

"The truth is that our finest moments are most likely to occur when we are feeling deeply uncomfortable, unhappy, or unfulfilled. For it is only in such moments, propelled by our discomfort, that we are likely to step out of our ruts and start searching for different ways to truer answers."

M. Scott Peck

You've gone through the "Awakening" Experience, released blocked energy using the "Forgiveness" Experience, and wrote down your new Prosperity Beliefs in the first few chapters. Now it's time for the "Clearing" Experience. This method is used to eliminate any remaining unconscious conflicts that could prohibit your ability to manifest dreams.

Perhaps your wish is to lose fifty pounds *and* continue eating all your favorite unhealthy snacks. It's a conflict because the two desires oppose one another. Eating healthy food, drinking more water, and enjoying regular fitness will ultimately produce improved health, self-confidence, and overall happiness. Yet, eating high-calorie junk food provides immediate gratification. How do you resolve the conflict? Use the "Clearing" Experience.

The easiest way to uncover a hidden conflict is by writing down what you want and what you're currently doing that prohibits the goal from being attained. Then, write down what the emotional payoffs are for both your desirable and undesirable behaviors. For instance, let's use the previous example of wanting to lose fifty pounds and eat junk food whenever you wish.

On a blank sheet of paper, write down both desires and then underneath, jot down the benefit or emotional payoff of each one. What are the pros of losing weight? What are the advantages of eating junk food? What are the positive benefits of each outcome? How would both of these positively serve you? Here's what it might look like:

I want to eat healthy food because...

a. I'll lose weight

b. Have more energy

c. My knees will stop hurting

d. I'll have more self-confidence

e. I won't get Type 2 diabetes like my mom

The unconscious payoff of eating healthy is feeling physically and emotionally happier while protecting oneself from future pain.

Now, what's the payoff for eating junk food?

a. It relaxes me

b. It feels like a reward at the end of a hard day

c. It distracts me when I'm bored

d. I don't feel deprived of what I want

The unconscious payoff of eating junk food is that it makes you feel emotionally happier when doing so.

Notice how both behaviors have similar intentions of producing emotional comfort. The "Clearing" Experience begins by asking a *new question*. How can I eat healthy while also feeling relaxed, rewarded, entertained, and satisfied? Asking the right questions unleashes your mind's creative power, and that's when brilliant answers are found.

Here are a few answers collected by hundreds of people who asked, "How can I lose fifty pounds without giving up all my favorite foods?"

a. I can view healthy food as a treat, reward, or new favorite food

b. Eating healthy food in smaller quantities increases my energy, which helps me pursue new adventures rather than hiding inside eating sugar

c. If bored, I will go for a walk, join a healthy cooking class, or try new hobbies

d. I still give myself permission to eat junk food occasionally, so I never feel deprived

This activity "clears out" hidden blocks by satisfying the unconscious driving need of both behaviors in a more empowering way.

Hidden Weight-Loss Blocks

I once coached a lovely woman named Virginia, who came into my office because she wanted to lose weight. We began upgrading her beliefs, releasing blocks, and retraining her mind to live happy and healthier. Over time, Virginia lost weight but struggled to reach her ideal goal.

One evening, I was facilitating a group coaching class. While people were coming in, I overheard Virginia having a conversation with some other guests. She was enthusiastically sharing her love of Southern cooking and how good she was in the kitchen. Virginia talked about her fried chicken and biscuits and gravy, and I could see she had put these listeners into an eating trance.

I walked over to the huddled group and asked Virginia to describe healthy food. She peered at me with a sad expression and said, "You mean rabbit food like carrots and celery?" I replied, "Virginia, you have an unconscious conflict that's prohibiting you from attaining your ideal weight. Your mind still associates tremendous pleasure to the fried foods that block you from losing the remaining pounds. You also describe healthy food as dull and boring."

I suggested describing healthy food in appealing and delicious ways and associating fried foods with fatigue and aging. Admittedly, when recommending this, Virginia glared at me like I was quite insane. Yet, my advice had already produced results for her, so she agreed. When I saw Virginia three weeks later, she had a big smile on her face. I asked why she was smiling, and she replied, "I'm down seven more pounds!" I congratulated her and asked how this happened.

She said, "Let me tell you about my vacation meals! I get out the beautiful wooden bowls I purchased in Hawaii and my fancy crystal glass. I fill my wooden bowl with beautiful greens and treats from my garden."

"What are your treats?"

"Oh, you know, my tomatoes, green peppers, and cucumbers. I cut up a big, juicy yellow lemon and toss it in my water. Child, it looks like a slice of sunshine! I feel like I'm at a spa vacation every time I eat."

I said, "Virginia, what about the fried chicken?"

She laughed and touched the sides of her face. "I haven't had that in weeks. It makes me feel all greasy inside."

Virginia had changed her story and cleared the inner conflict. She could still feel special and in charge of her meals yet do so in a manner that also satisfied her desire to lose weight. She found a new way to meet her emotional needs, and the results were so visible, she could see them in the mirror.

HIDDEN MONEY BLOCKS

Growing up, I always felt provided for. Yet, when I moved out on my own, I barely got by. I worked midnights at a truck stop, sold vacuum cleaners door-to-door, and even got a job at RadioShack while trying to sell these new machines called computers. While going through college, I began working as a mental health technician at various inpatient and outpatient facilities.

In 1995, I graduated with a master's degree. I then opened a small hypnosis practice using the tiny front room of my rundown apartment. It still amazes me that people showed up for sessions at that place. Because I was living paycheck to paycheck, I figured everybody else did as well and charged hardly anything for my hypnosis coaching. It was $35 a session or two for $60. What a bargain! Making $30 an hour felt exciting, but not if you only saw four or five clients per month. Somehow, I just always squeaked by with my bills each month.

During the Midwestern winters, my heating bill would sometimes be higher than my rent. I remember buying a ton of cheap candles at garage sales in the summertime and lighting them all in my bedroom during the winter to stay a little warmer. To this day, I thank God that the apartment didn't catch on fire. I guess the asbestos in the walls did their job. I had to get more clients, raise my prices, or perhaps do both. But I didn't know how to get more clients, and I also had a hidden conflict about money. So, I decided to attend my first hypnosis conference to see what other hypnotists were doing to grow their practices.

I hid in the back of the room so nobody would call on me and took as many notes as possible. It was inspiring to hear the results people were helping their clients achieve with a wide variety of goals. Hypnotherapy is a worthy profession filled with kindhearted people who have done so much good in the world. Yet, most of the people at that conference struggled with making a full-time living as a hypnotist in the same way I did, mostly because we all had the same hidden conflict about money.

We had either started out with humble beginnings or felt that charging someone for the beautiful work we produced somehow tainted the process. Of course, that was nonsense, but many of us struggled with this perception. I'd hear lectures from those who'd cleared their hidden blocks sharing how they were charging $100, $150, and even $250 for a single session, and I could as well if I produced the results the client was there for. I thought this was amazing but was skeptical. Were they telling the truth or just putting on a show?

I was faced with a decision. Chose to believe this was possible for me as well or tell myself it wasn't and remain broke. During one of the lectures, the trainer said something that's stuck with me ever since. *Your self-worth determines your net worth, and you decide what your time is worth.* He went on to say that you're not charging by the hour, but for the positive outcome. When somebody comes to you to stop smoking, how much is being a non-smoker worth to that individual? How much would you pay not to get lung cancer or emphysema or carry an oxygen tank around with you? What is that worth? The average smoker spends $60,000 or more, over 30 years of smoking, only to have significant health problems. Does it make sense to feel guilty about charging $300 to help them quit?

I never thought about it like that before, and never would have if I hadn't gotten out of my comfort zone and attended that conference. If all you have are your own opinions, you'll never reach your fullest potential. You must get feedback from others to make better-educated decisions. I considered raising my prices from $30 to $50 a session. But then I attended another lecture and was challenged to push myself much farther than I was comfortable going.

The speaker said, "In many ways, we are like a rubber band. The more we are stretched, the more enormous our potential to fly becomes when released. The problem is that when the rubber band hits the ground, it retakes its original shape. Your goal is to continually stretch yourself, so you don't revert back to where you started."

I decided to raise my prices to $100 per session because that totally pushed me out of my comfort zone. It's why I'm so fond of saying today that your most significant breakthroughs are always hidden in the places you don't want to go. How I marketed my services also got an overhaul. I began telling potential clients that I didn't charge by the hour. Instead, they were paying for an outcome that ultimately was much more valuable than the price they were paying. This message was well-received because it made sense.

My desire to help people and the exciting results they experienced were still the same. Yet, how I internally felt about receiving payment shifted. I had cleared the first hidden block about money and felt good about being paid more. Of course, if you were reading carefully, you noticed that I said only the first block about making money had been removed. Like how much money I felt capable or worthy of earning in a year. Other hidden blocks would also have to be uncovered and cleared several times before I began attracting greater prosperity.

Eventually, I hired a coach who taught me the value of spending more time with clients than trying to solve all their problems in a couple of sessions. I was trained to sell hypnosis packages that were ten times more expensive than offering a one-time meeting. I remember being so nervous the first time I provided the costliest package I had to a client. I was scared to death that she would laugh in my face and storm out the door, along with the money for rent that month.

Instead, she smiled and said, "Will you accept a check?" I almost fainted! My heart was pounding so hard I wasn't sure I could reply. Smiling, I nodded as I watched her write that check and hand it to me. She might have given me a million dollars because that's what it felt like at the time. I was used to getting paid for single sessions and suddenly received a check for ten sessions up front. I could pay all the bills, put some money into savings, and still have enough to take my lady to Red Lobster. All because I cleared a hidden block by associating pleasure to being paid more.

Let's break this down. I did not feel comfortable asking for more money because I had a belief that it diminished the spiritual work I was doing. This limiting belief came from the idea that having a lot of money made you a greedy or selfish person, which many broke people subscribe to. But it wasn't just that. I was afraid that people would leave me if I asked for something more for myself. There was a deep-seated fear of abandonment and embarrassment that took many years to uncover and heal.

I was providing life-changing services that helped people eliminate needless emotional suffering, which felt wonderful. On the other end, if I ask for more compensation, nobody would work with me. There have been so many occasions where I asked for less than what my services were worth simply because I was afraid of hearing the word "No."

I've always had a strong desire to help people because of my personal experience with unnecessary suffering. If there were a way I could help people avoid that same type of pain, I would provide it. I also wanted to earn more money so that I didn't have to feel stressed out about it. I hated taking my girlfriend, who is now my wife of twenty-five years, out to dinner only to worry about what she was going to order. Having a feeling of security and inner peace around money was something I desperately desired.

Eventually, I figured out that I could feel good about myself, serve others, and be financially prosperous all at the same time. I also realized that the more value you bring to the world, the more valuable you become. I finally felt safe enough to ask for what I wanted. If someone said no, somebody else would say, "Yes!" People are happy to pay for something they get tremendous value from. Plus, the more people invest in coaching programs, the more committed they become to achieving their goals. My net worth increased because my self-worth went up first. The most amazing part is that I was the one who was ultimately in charge of both, and so are you.

In Stephen Covey's classic business book, *The 7 Habits of Highly Effective People*, his seventh habit was to create synergy. He explained that compromise is when two parties who enter a negotiation both feel they must give up or sacrifice some of what they want to make the deal happen. However, synergy is when two parties come together, seeking a new option that neither had considered on their own. This third option improves the deal on both sides and gives people more than they expected in the first place.

You are creating synergy by resolving hidden conflicts. Instead of limiting yourself to all-or-nothing thinking, seek out the synergistic option. For instance, resist believing you can only lose weight if you stop eating sugar forever. Instead, imagine occasionally satisfying your sweet tooth, yet enjoying a healthier lifestyle more because of how good it keeps you feeling. You end up with *more* than you bargained for initially. It's a win-win!

Goal-Achieving Blocks

Several years ago, I decided to provide more leadership keynotes to help average supervisors and managers transform into mesmerizing leaders. The coach I hired to help me with this suggested I start regularly calling upon organizations to let them know about my programs. I agreed to begin doing so the next day. Yet, when that day arrived, I found myself occupied by other activities. I put it off until the following day, but it didn't happen then either.

I had fallen into the trap of "doing it tomorrow," and I'd learned from hundreds of clients that tomorrow never comes. Thus, I sat down and went through the "Clearing" Experience to figure out why I was procrastinating. It turns out I wasn't so much afraid of people yelling at me or being rude. Most of the time, people are quite friendly if you provide them upfront value, rather than asking for a favor.

I wrote down my desirable behavior and goal, making regular telephone prospecting calls and delivering more public keynotes. Underneath, I jotted down reasons for wanting this, such as having the desire to add more value to the world and make a more considerable impact in a shorter amount of time. This would also produce more clients, income, and emotional security that emanates from financial prosperity. The underlying positive intention for me was emotional security.

Next, it was time to figure out the hidden payoff for procrastinating on those prospecting calls. It turns out I was subconsciously resentful about having to call people and "beg them" to have me speak to their people. It felt like I had more than paid my dues, and at this point in my career, people should be requesting me to come to their conferences. Yes, there is a lot of self-pity and entitlement in those beliefs, but I wanted to be honest with you so that you will be honest with yourself.

I decided to employ synergy to the situation by exploring how I could make those calls *and* have the experience of people being excited to work with me. This created a flood of ideas for adding tremendous upfront value, which would then spur more invitations to present. In the upcoming chapters, you'll learn how to program your Unconscious Mind to provide ways of attaining your goals faster than by using logic (your Conscious Mind) alone.

I could also improve my stage skills, so those who saw me speak at one event would invite me to speak at theirs. I wouldn't have to make as many prospecting calls and could build up my speaking dates over time using natural momentum. Because I applied synergy to resolve hidden blocks, my mind now associated pleasure to prospecting calls. Joe Vitale always says that "money loves speed," so I decided to pick up the phone and make my first call.

I reached out to a local Rotary group. When telling the nice woman who answered about my hypnosis background and program topics, she seemed excited and asked to schedule a meeting in person. This was just the response I'd hoped for. It immediately reinforced my new belief that making those "friendship calls" would be a joyful experience. It also strengthened my belief that miracles happen when you go within and upgrade self-limiting beliefs. If you learn to go within, you'll never go without.

I provided many programs for Rotary clubs and continued polishing my presentation skills, which resulted in my being asked to keynote at an International Rotary convention. Before I knew it, my calendar filled with speaking gigs for other non-profit organizations like Kiwanis, the Optimists Club, and dozens more. All of this occurred because I took the time to clear blocks and gain clarity on what I really wanted. Then, I took consistent action while preparing myself for the opportunities to come. This is the ultimate formula for success:

Preparation + Opportunity = Success

"CLEARING" EXPERIENCE

It's time to clear hidden conflicts you may have. Use the space below or grab a piece of paper and write a desirable behavior or goal. Then write why you want this. What's the positive intention for behaving in this way, or achieving that goal?

Next, write the current behaviors that are getting in the way of you attaining that desirable goal. Also, jot down the positive intentions for behaving in this way. How do those behaviors protect you, reduce stress, or comfort you?

Now contemplate how you might use synergy to satisfy both desires in a more empowering way. Be creative and write lots of ideas for how this might be accomplished.

Once you've identified your new approach, imagine it happening the way you want it to, and allow those feelings of peace or enthusiasm to fill you up inside. What if all the things you wish for came true? How would you feel? Experience those feelings now and connect them to the behaviors that will transform these wishes into reality. Then, describe what you're experiencing or realizing below.

Now move! Miracles also love speed. The faster you take action on that which you desire, the quicker things begin to unfold. Carpe diem (seize the day)! Write what your first couple of moves will be.

Watch For Clues + Take Action Quickly = Winning Life!

CHAPTER 10
THE BILLIONAIRE'S SECRET

*"You are the only problem you will ever have,
and you are the only solution!"*

Bob Proctor, author of *It's Not About the Money*

Congratulations! You've come a long way, as few travel this far down the path. I'm sure the personal discoveries and breakthroughs you've experienced are already worthwhile, yet I want to reward you for your courage and commitment to this journey.

Most books would end here. You'd get a "good luck and best wishes" pat on the back and be instructed to put what you've learned into action. But what if you apply all this wisdom and still struggle to turn your biggest dreams into reality? What's the next step after upgrading self-limiting beliefs, clearing emotional blocks, and taking intentional action for many years? Is there some missing secret that you somehow missed? Or are some people just luckier than others? The rest of this journey together is dedicated to answering those questions. What you're about to learn is profound, and very few people on this planet have heard or genuinely understand the insights and principles you are about to acquire.

You can only grow so far on your own. To reach the next level of awareness, success, fortune, or happiness, you will need a coach or mentor. There are a variety of coaches out there who can help you attain your goals and dreams. The best way to find a coach is by seeking out someone who has already achieved the goal you wish to reach. Next, check their testimonials. Just because someone can accomplish a goal doesn't mean they are a good coach or teacher. Of course, you can call my office, and my team will assist you.

There was one person I knew who could help me uncover the missing secret if there was such a thing, and it was Dr. Joe Vitale. If you've read Joe's books (there are dozens to choose from), you'll quickly realize his life has been devoted to uncovering the mysteries of personal growth and spiritual enlightenment. His journey has taken him from being homeless at one point to living the rich and famous lifestyle. He now hangs out with millionaires and billionaires and shares what he's learned about manifesting your wildest dreams with people worldwide.

As fate would have it, I met Joe at the first hypnosis convention I attended some twenty years ago. He had a booth and was selling his best-selling courses on hypnotic marketing. I didn't know anything about Joe, but I noticed two things. First, the most famous speakers at the event were hanging out at Joe's booth. Second, when I approached him, he was warm and friendly. Some successful businesspeople can be snobby or distant. Not Joe. He was happy to start a conversation. He even gave me his cell number if I ever had a question. Little did I know that, years later, I'd be watching one of the most successful documentaries of all time, *The Secret,* and see Joe as one of the featured experts!

I hadn't been in contact with Joe for years and was curious to see if his cell phone number had transferred into my smartphone after all this time. I began scrolling through my address book, and there he was. Then I wondered if the number still worked. That would be a miracle. I was a little nervous about calling, so I decided to send a quick text. No response. Well, it was worth a shot. But the next day, there was a reply! *Hi Tim, I'm in Russia.*

Reach out in a couple weeks. Joe. I couldn't believe it. I marked it on my calendar to reach back out, and when I did, another reply came through. *In Spain, speaking. Reach out next week. Adios!* I did, and we scheduled a telephone call for the following week. It was great catching up with Joe, and I wanted to spend more time with him. I asked if he would be a guest on my *How to Be Mesmerizing* podcast. He agreed, and I was thrilled. Finally, I was going to get some answers to questions that puzzled me for years.

This interview led to many more conversations with Dr. Joe. I'll be sharing those private conversations and the incredible insights gained from him in the remaining chapters. Buckle up, my friend. It's about to get inspiring! As Joe likes to say, "Upward and onward!"

INTERVIEW WITH DR. JOE VITALE

"Joe, how did you go from poverty to prosperity?"

"Tim, I would say what got me here is everything from persistence to continually working on myself. It's self-improvement, optimism, hope, mentors, friends, and people who believed in me before I believed in myself. So many people ask what I did to go from homeless to wealthy. They are all looking for the magic pill as if there's one magic answer. It frustrated the hell out of me until I realized I do know the answer. Here's the one thing: I did everything! I read all the books, listened to the audios, attended the seminars, hired coaches, and found mentors. I soaked it all up. Not everything I learned worked or helped, but I believed that all of it was moving me forward—and it did."

"Joe, that is one of the most honest answers I've ever heard. Experts are often trying to sell something, so they have that one system, the one thing that's going to make it happen for you. But you're saying there isn't one thing. Even if a particular approach worked for one person, it doesn't mean it will work for you. There is no one-size-fits-all magic solution. That's been my experience too. I've hustled for years, trying everything to keep growing, earning, and experiencing. I have put all kinds of irons in the fire and hooks in the water. What's going to bite? Cause you don't know what's going to hit. You just have to keep testing, testing, testing, until something clicks. Is that right?"

"That's it," said Joe.

"Joe, I understand that persistence is one of the keys to personal development and financial success. Keep trying new things, hire new coaches, and continually move forward. Yet, it feels like that's what a coach might say to keep a client busy because they don't really know what the solution is for them."

Joe smiled and replied, "I'm going to take the opportunity to inject what I think is the most crucial bit of wisdom here. Yes, being persistent and taking action are definitely part of the formula. What I've learned is that you must also take care of the inside of you, so you are in alignment to receive success. When I lived in poverty, which lasted about ten years, I was doing all the persistence stuff and taking action. I was writing, sending out my writing to publishers, and working on myself. But what I didn't know at that time is that my inner beliefs about deservingness, success, money, and self-worth weren't there. All of the stuff I was doing was part of the formula. But the other part was that I was shooting myself in the foot because I wasn't mentally ready to receive money, success, publication, or any of the things I was striving for."

> ***"You have to take care of the inside of you—your beliefs about self-worth, money, and deservedness—so you are in alignment to receive success."***
> Dr. Joe Vitale

Joe continued. "This is what I've been calling the missing secret, and it's what sabotages many who struggle with applying the Law of Attraction. All the self-help stuff out there tends to miss this one thing. Believe me, I am a self-help junkie. I've read the books, listened to the audio courses, purchased hundreds of other people's products, and have applied the lessons for decades.

I realized we have a conscious mind, subconscious mind, unconscious mind, collective unconscious, and that the data that's most heavily influencing your success is sitting below the conscious realm. Consciously we say, 'I'm going to be a success. I'm going to be an author. I'm going to open my business, and I'm going to rake in sales.' But unconsciously, if you think money is evil, success will corrupt you, or you're not smart enough to pull this all off, you'll subconsciously sabotage yourself. If you have a subconscious belief that 'I'm not good enough, skilled enough, likable, lovable, worthy, or that things don't work out for me,' that will become your reality."

The missing secret is realizing your unconscious beliefs shape your life far more than any other factor!

Joe leaned in with a serious expression and continued. "Most have an entire database of limiting negative thoughts stored in their brains, and until those are cleaned up, we'll go in the right direction but sabotage our own efforts and won't even know it. I did that for ten years until my own awakening, if you will, and I started to realize, *Oh my God, I'm creating all of my life from my unconscious beliefs, not the conscious beliefs!* When you get in there and clean them up (the unconscious beliefs), you have alignment and integrity. Then when you say, 'I'm going to go do something,' you can go do it and achieve it. I want to make sure that we don't deceive anybody because it's all about taking action. Yes, putting in the work is part of the formula. But this inside work—what I call taking care of the counter intentions—is also a vital part of the equation. Put those together, and now success is almost guaranteed. You still have other variables to deal with, but you'll be moving in the right direction with greater force and clarity."

I pondered Joe's description of subconscious counter intentions. Then replied, "This makes a lot of sense, Joe. The documentary, *The Secret*, reveals that what you think about most of the time becomes your life. After the film came out, the most prominent critics said you couldn't just think yourself successful. You must also take action. However, there is a third step, what you're referring to as the missing secret. You must also upgrade your unconscious beliefs, so they are in alignment with your desired outcome."

Step 1: Intentionally and consciously focus on what you want.

Step 2: Take consistent action to attain the desired outcome, gain feedback, and adjust on the fly.

Step 3: Make sure unconscious beliefs are in alignment with the desired outcome.

For much of my coaching career, I led people through those steps in that order. Yet, about ten years ago, I started heavily focusing on Step 3. I've found that your unconscious beliefs have the most influence over your conscious thoughts and behaviors. Trying to get people to think positive or feel motivated without upgrading those underlying beliefs first was futile. I wanted to go deeper with this, so I asked Joe more questions.

I said, "What if someone has worked hard to improve their conscious and unconscious beliefs, and also feels that abundance and prosperity are good because of the good deeds you can do with them? Yet, things still haven't fallen into place when attaining that one big dream, whether it's making a million dollars, losing one hundred pounds, or being in a genuinely happy relationship. What's their next move?"

"Well," said Joe, "if they are still not attaining the results they prefer, I think it's a sign that they are incomplete with that inner work on themselves. In my worldview, we get precisely what we unconsciously believe and expect to receive. We experience what we *unconsciously* believe and expect. I meet people who say things like, 'Hey, I watched *The Secret*. I liked the message, but you know, the Law of Attraction, affirmations, or visualization doesn't work for me.' And I'll say, 'Oh, really? Do you ever worry?' They will undoubtedly reply, 'Oh yeah, I worry all the time.' I reply, 'Well, if you worry, you're practicing visualization. You're practicing affirmations and proving the Law of Attraction and everything that goes with it, but you're doing it unconsciously and blindly to produce your undesirable results.'"

Worrying uses the Law of Attraction to draw what you don't want into your life.

Joe continued. "The very first thing I tell people is we have to wake up to the fact that we're creating our own reality. You may be creating it unknowingly and unconsciously at the moment. If you're still struggling in your business, you probably still have limiting beliefs about yourself, your business, or money. We can't blame it on circumstances, politics, or the current environment because there are too many examples of people who are succeeding despite it. Those prevailing are proving that all of us can thrive even in the most challenging circumstances with the right beliefs. What I always say is its mirror work. We need to look in the mirror and be ruthlessly honest with ourselves about our beliefs.

"I have also found that it's easy to deceive ourselves of our true beliefs, and the only solution is to test your views through the help of others. Whether it's a coach, mentor, or mastermind group, you need to be with other people who can see or hear your beliefs and hold up a mirror to you in a loving, nonjudgmental way. They allow you to look at your self-limiting ideas, and especially those you didn't realize were there. Every one of us is living from our deep-seated assumptions, but most don't know it."

It's easy to deceive ourselves of our true beliefs, and the only solution is to test your views through the help of others.

I knew what Joe said was one hundred percent accurate. Even the famous author of *Think and Grow Rich*, Napoleon Hill, said that what the world's most successful people had in common was that they all belonged to a mastermind group. Self-deception is the most prominent detriment to achievement because it's near impossible to recognize your own blind spots. As one of my coaches used to say, "You can't see the label when you're in the bottle." The thing that really landed for me was when Joe said it's easy to deceive yourself. The moment Joe spoke those words, a memory flashed through my mind about a brief interview I had with a potential new coach.

She was highly recommended to me, so I reached out. She asked about my goals and where I was struggling. I answered her questions, and the response was, "I can hear some self-limiting beliefs that are likely holding you back." Arrogantly, I dismissed her comments because I was the "expert" in unconscious beliefs. Thus, this couldn't be the issue. I wanted her to give me a new million-dollar marketing technique, not advice on upgrading beliefs. The irony is hilarious, I know. I have a sheepish grin on my face as I share this with you. That was a costly lesson because I did not move forward with her. Nor did I even ask her what the beliefs were that she picked up on. Ugh!

Here are the two bits of wisdom I gained from that experience. First, when you ask a coach for advice, take the feedback and implement it. Don't debate whether you agree with it or not. Why hire a coach if you are simply going to do what you were doing in the first place? Second, always seek out hidden beliefs that may be sabotaging your efforts before attempting a new marketing technique. The right expectations can make any marketing technique more fruitful, and the wrong views will undermine the best of strategies.

When you ask a coach for advice, take the feedback and implement it. Otherwise, why hire a coach?

"Tim," Joe said, "sustainable success is experienced through tremendous self-awareness. My most significant breakthroughs in life came when I started working with a coach because it's one thing to read and even write self-help books, but it's another thing to work with somebody listening to your story, looking for your beliefs, and feeding them back to you. Your world is formed by your subjective experiences, even though most tend to think they are dealing with the same reality as everyone else. It'll seem like concrete, unchangeable truth, but life is fluid, and much of what we perceive is an optical illusion. What we're seeing is based on the beliefs that are in our heads. Having somebody that's on the outside of my brain saying, 'Hey, have you ever considered this?' is incredibly valuable. Once an unconscious belief is revealed, an entirely new set of possibilities open to you that weren't accessible before. I'm a great believer in having coaches, mentors, being in a mastermind, and having people who can support you."

"Joe, were there any beliefs that you started out with that you no longer buy into anymore?"

"The biggest one for me, Tim, was the belief that you have to really struggle and go through the drama of hopelessness as a kind of a curriculum to become a successful author, which was my life's dream. I swear that was a fundamental operating belief, and I had no conscious awareness that it was there. When I suddenly realized this, it made sense that I would subconsciously think this way because the authors I most admired at that time, like Jack London and Ernest Hemingway, had dramatic lives that ended in suicide. Jack London was as successful as they come. He wrote fifty books but died before the age of forty. I thought that I had to have a life like theirs to have success like theirs. When I realized, wow, I can model their writing style but not their lifestyle and can be far more successful by dropping that other belief; that was huge.

"Another one for me—and I find most people have this one—is the idea that I'm not good enough. Most people grew up in an environment where they had well-meaning parents, but I've often said, were your parents enlightened? Probably not. They had plenty of their own baggage and limiting beliefs, and they downloaded a lot of that into you. You end up feeling like you're less than, or not smart, attractive, courageous, or lovable enough to receive unconditional affection. That sense of not being good enough will unconsciously stop you from achieving, and especially receiving, the success you want. Thus, this was another belief I had to look at and say, 'Hey, I am good enough. I am lovable. I am likable, and I do accept myself.' Every person on this planet operates from a belief system, and some of their deepest beliefs may not be serving them well. Thus, I invite everybody to look in the mirror and ask yourself, 'What is it that I truly want, and do my current beliefs support this?'

What is it that I truly want, and do my current beliefs support this?

I smiled. "Those are powerful questions, Joe."

"Yes. It's like being a mind detective who's digging out the beliefs that are creating the lifestyle you have. This is exhilarating work because you end up freeing yourself. Forty years ago, I looked out at the world and felt it was against me. I was scared and angry, and I didn't see opportunities, goals, or possibilities. It was so dark. Years later, I'm the same guy. It's the same brain and body, same universe, same ability to make choices and decisions. Yet, when I look out into the world, I see a life of magic and miracles. I see abundance, prosperity, and opportunities all around me. It's exhilarating! What's changed? My beliefs, how I speak to myself, and what I tell myself each day."

"That's exactly right!" I exclaimed. "I've helped thousands of lifelong dieters lose weight and improve their health and happiness without the struggle of dieting. People think it's the hypnotic trances I help people enter, but that's not it. I use hypnosis to help people uncover their self-sabotaging beliefs, and when we upgrade them, the emotional and physical weight melts away almost effortlessly.

"I once provided coaching for a woman named Kathleen. She lost 155 pounds in ten months. We were having the same conversation the other day, and she said the same thing you just did: 'When I look in the mirror, my body looks so different, but it's still me looking back. The only thing I did differently from all the diets in the past was to change my beliefs about myself, so I finally felt worthy of loving me.' I recall the first time Kathleen and I met. She complained that she couldn't lose weight no matter how many times she tried and asked if I could help her be a *happy* fat person. Then Kathleen began to cry because she was settling for less than what she really wanted. I knew what was possible for her, even though she didn't believe it. Kathleen's on the other side of a once-impossible dream now and has become the exact person she always wanted to be. This was the direct result of having the courage to do her mirror work."

"That's a wonderful example, Tim. I also regularly see limiting beliefs people have when it comes to accumulating wealth. It's why four out of five people who win millions of dollars in the lottery are back to being broke or where they financially started within five years. If you're not ready for wealth, haven't accepted that money is a useful tool, have issues with deservingness, or struggle with others' opinions, they'll subconsciously find a way to get rid of the money. Many go bankrupt as the rest of the world wonders how that's possible. It's mind-boggling how someone could go from being broke to being a millionaire and then broke again. Yet, it's just another demonstration that we have to take care of the inner for the outer to be sustainable."

"Joe, because of your success as an author and speaker, you're hanging around with others who have attained a high level of financial success. Are there any inside secrets the rich and famous are privy to that everyone else is unaware of?"

"That is a great question," replied Joe. "I love it because I'm now hanging around people that are billionaires. I'm not a billionaire yet, but I'm headed there," he said with a smile. "One of the most recent billionaires I've met is a young fellow from Sweden who now resides in Thailand. He shared with me that he was also homeless at one point, sleeping on benches next to the ocean. Desperate and hungry, he found a way to call a friend back home in Sweden and ask for money. But his friend did something I'm not sure I could do. Instead of sending money, he mailed him a book. Let's stop and think. My friend in Thailand is starving. He has nothing, and his friend says, 'I'm not going to send you any money. I'm going to send you a book. It's called *The Secret.* Read it and apply what you learn.'

"Now, Andres, my friend in Thailand, is angry. He didn't want a book, yet when it arrived, he read it to see why his friend thought it was more important to send that than money for food. He decided to prove the principles wrong by putting them to the test. First, he thought, *I'll try to manifest a cup of coffee.* Two days later, he received a cup of coffee. Surprised, he thought, *Let me try to manifest a lunch.* A day or so later, he received lunch. Then he thought, *Let me try to manifest an apartment.* A couple of weeks later, he found himself residing in an apartment. Andres continued attempting to manifest things, and fifteen years later, he's become a billionaire. Oh, did I mention he's only thirty-five years old?

"I had the privilege of meeting Andres because he said Jack Canfield, Bob Proctor, and Joe Vitale were the three people who changed his life. He brought me to Thailand and had me speak at his event. Later, I had the idea of putting his story into a book and sharing his eighteen success principles. Just like I tell others, when you have a moment of inspiration, act on it immediately. After a lengthy conversation, he agreed to have me write this book for him. I got to hear his whole story in detail and how he went from homeless to billionaire, which happens to be the title of the book. He also shared how to attract wealth and become a money magnet. So, yes, I know what those inside secrets are that wealthy people apply to attract abundance and prosperity. Of course, they aren't really secrets. The principles are talked about all the time. The difference is whether you consistently believe in and apply those principles. Most do not, but those who do feel like they found a magic lamp and the power to make wishes come true."

Most success principles aren't really secrets. If you want them to work in your life, you must believe in and apply them.

"Joe, can you share some of these wealth principles and how Andres became a billionaire?"

"Sure. They're basic principles like visualizing what you want, using daily affirmations, and upgrading your beliefs using the book's exercises. It's also crucial to take massive action toward what you want and view setbacks as feedback rather than failures. But there was one principle that blew my mind, and I want to share it with you now. In Thailand, on people's birthdays, they don't receive gifts; they give them. Never in my life had I considered that I'd be the one giving gifts on my birthday. I was born in December and resented it because people would say, 'Here's your Christmas present *and* your birthday present.' Yet, Andres said that they have a gift culture mentality in Thailand, so on his birthday, he'd generously give to others. Shortly afterward, he noticed his income steadily increasing. The more charitable he was to others, the more his wealth increased. Then he shared how he manifested his first million dollars.

"Andres heard about a small village that had children with HIV. The caregivers there were doing their best to help these kids, but their facility was rundown, and they had very few resources. Andres decided to donate $80,000 to that place. Now remember, he's not a billionaire or even a millionaire yet. At the time, this was a vast financial stretch for him, but Andres donated the money anyway because it was a worthy cause. But he didn't just write a check. Andres also gave a lot of his own labor by painting walls, pounding nails, etc. Within a month of selflessly serving others, he professionally landed the largest deal of his life for $1,080,000. Wow! He got his investment back and a million extra dollars.

Jack Canfield, famous co-author of the *Chicken Soup for the Soul* series, is writing a book about billionaires right now and said there are three things they all have in common. They regularly exercise, meditate, and donate to charities."

> ***"The secret to living is giving."***
> Tony Robbins

"Joe, what about those who they feel they've given a lot, but haven't seen a windfall return like Andres?"

"Yeah, that's a great question, Tim, and to me, the answer is obvious. You can give all the money, time, and energy you want. But if you quietly hold resentments about money or the lack of it, your flow of abundance will be blocked. Also, many are comfortable with giving. Yet, you must also be open to receiving for it to come back. Andres doesn't have any of those blocks, so the money's abundantly going out and flowing in. He's doing massive deals with giant corporations and becoming a dominant force because he generously gives and receives. He has overcome the internal blocks that kept him in poverty. Most who are not born rich have issues with money and need to do the mirror work to clear those blocks. I've met numerous people who were happy to give, yet had problems receiving any form of compensation back, even if it was a thank you. Unconsciously, they were plagued by ideas that money, or any type of adulation, tarnished their good deeds."

Joe's energy heightened as he passionately shared the revelations that take people from rags to riches. "Tim, to those who feel they are not abundantly receiving, I invite them to really look at the results they're getting and ask what beliefs might trigger that outcome. Ask yourself, 'If money isn't filling my pockets or bank accounts, what thoughts do I dwell on that could be preventing this?' It could be anything from 'Money is the root of all evil' to 'This works for everybody else, but it doesn't work for me.' Whatever it is, it's just a belief and not a fact. It's not even real.

"Andres set out to prove the teachings in *The Secret* wrong. He came from a place of skepticism. Andres was starving in his reality, and the idea that he'd end up a billionaire was outrageous. Yet—and this is one of the things that's also important to do—he slowly began going for some of the things he wanted. He didn't start testing the success principles by trying to become a billionaire. That wasn't even in the realm of possibility based upon his belief system at the time. He started by manifesting a cup of coffee. Then lunch. Then a job. Then another job, which led to an apartment, and more importantly, to a new set of beliefs about what's possible. Those possibilities and the potential were inside him the whole time, even when he went to sleep on a bench at night hungry. This potential is inside all of us right now. The trick is to believe it or at least to have the courage to test it out. Who knows? Maybe you will be the next billionaire."

If money isn't filling my pockets or bank accounts, what thoughts do I dwell on that could be preventing this?

"Joe, Andres has an amazing story, but do you think some people just get lucky? Mark Cuban is a billionaire, and during an interview, he was asked if he had to do it all over, would he become a billionaire again. Mark replied, 'Hell no, I wouldn't become a billionaire. Do you know how lucky you have to be for that to happen? You must be born in the right country, at the right time in history, with the right idea, and all these other things that would have to fall right into place. Don't get me wrong. I'd still become a millionaire and be successful. But there is a large factor of luck when it comes to becoming a billionaire.' So, do you think that some people are just luckier than others in this game of life?" Joe's response rocked me once more.

"That's an interesting question. I dare to answer because there's a hint of victimhood in the question itself. If I say yes, some people are luckier, it sounds like there's this random astrological power based on the alignment of the planets or something in your background or DNA that predicts whether you'll be lucky. But I don't believe that. Instead, I feel we live in a belief-driven universe. Change your beliefs, and you'll experience a different type of world. If some are luckier than others and you want to be one of those lucky people, start believing you already are. 'I'm the luckiest person on the planet!' Anything is possible, my friend."

> **"We live in a belief-driven universe. Change your beliefs, and you'll experience a different type of world. If some are luckier than others and you want to be one of those lucky people, start believing you already are."**
> Dr. Joe Vitale

"Mirror-Work" Experience

1. What is it that I truly want?

2. Do my current beliefs support this?

3. What beliefs would support this?

CHAPTER 11

SIX STEPS FOR MANIFESTING ANYTHING

"You control your future, your destiny.
What you think about comes about.
By recording your dreams and goals on paper,
you set in motion the process of becoming the person you most want to be. Put your future in good hands—your own."

Mark Victor & Crystal Hansen, Co-Authors of *Ask!*

The other day, I recorded a podcast interview with Jordan Carnduff. We talked about how people form their identities and whether it was possible for someone to change their sense of self. (If you'd like to hear the conversation, subscribe to my *How to Be Mesmerizing* podcast at MesmerizingPodcast.com.) During our discussion, Jordan remarked that I'm always taking information and putting it into an actionable plan. That is true because knowledge without action is a waste of wisdom. Plus, I've always wished there was a specific path to follow that would consistently produce positive outcomes. Too often, I was willing to do whatever it took to succeed, but I just didn't know what steps to take. Over the last fifty years, I've uncovered a few of the paths that produce consistently positive results. I'm excited to share with you the one for manifesting your wildest dreams.

The following six steps will allow you to manifest your heart's desires, as long as it's good (healthy, safe) for you and those around you. By that, I mean, if you wish to play on your favorite NFL team and you're sixty years old, this is physically not good for your health, or right for the other players who might feel guilty about putting you in the hospital. However, other things could happen that you hadn't considered. You might end up working for the team in some capacity, meeting your favorite players, sitting in a box seat during a home game, or standing on the field during the halftime show. Of course, with video games and virtual reality systems, you can also virtually play for your favorite team. It's often not the dream, but what you believe will happen as a result of having this experience that's most desired. Ask yourself why you want to play for that team, and write down as many reasons as possible to unmask what you're trying to accomplish by attaining this goal. Once you've done this, you'll be able to satisfy those subconscious needs, which is good for you and everyone else. I've just revealed Step 1 in the manifesting formula.

Six Steps for Manifesting Anything

1. Identify and clarify what you want to manifest or attract into your life and why
2. Clear all negative (self-limiting) beliefs
3. Feel your intention already achieved
4. Watch for clues, speedily act upon them as they appear, and adjust on the fly
5. Let go and be needless
6. Live in the moment with gratitude

Let's break these steps down so you can start implementing them right away.

Step 1: Identify and clarify what you want to manifest or attract into your life and why

One of the most common stumbling blocks is defining what you want to manifest because most people are too focused on what they don't want, what's missing, or what they don't like. Let's use this to your advantage. Begin by identifying an initial goal or dream you'd like to attain. Next, clarify how you'd like this dream to be experienced by first writing down what you don't want to happen. Here's an example.

"I want a million dollars."

- I don't want it to be a horrible struggle attaining the money.
- Or cost me my marriage.
- Or take twenty years to accumulate.
- Or it to be taken away because of taxes.
- Or for it to come from a life insurance policy because I died!

"Why do I want a million dollars?"

- I will feel important.
- I will know I can accomplish anything!
- Others will respect me.
- I will have the freedom to travel wherever I want.
- I can buy my dream car.
- I can make an impact on my favorite charity.

"What's currently preventing me from having a million dollars?"

- I don't believe it's possible because it hasn't happened, even though I've worked hard for a long time.
- My spouse spends too much money.
- I don't know what to do to make it happen.
- I'm older now and feel like time is running out.
- The economy has tanked because of COVID-19.

"What must I believe to net a million dollars in the way that's right for me?"

- I am already a millionaire in my mind and heart. It's happened for many others who believed, and now it's occurring for me as well.
- I don't have to know all the answers and can trust in God and my unconscious mind to lead me down the right path.
- I'm already important and believe I can accomplish whatever I want.
- Others already respect me, not for my net worth, but because of how I care about and serve others.
- I'm already blessed, grateful, and abundant.
- I'm investing in my education and myself, so I know how to put my money to work in a manner that causes it to multiply naturally.
- I'm comfortable and happy with money flowing in and out of my life.
- I'm excited about sharing my time, energy, and money to improve the lives of others.

- I am always watching for opportunities, expecting them to appear, quickly taking action on them, and feeling gratitude because I'm aware of being able to play in this magical universe.
- Life can be difficult, and I'm okay with that.

What does a day in your life look, sound, and feel like now that you've attained the goal? (Write down how this improves your confidence, decision-making abilities, creativity, motivation, health, relationships, communication skills, and overall fulfillment.)

"I get up in the morning feeling excited for the day. I have set other goals for myself and have the confidence to reach them as well. I'm more relaxed and make time to eat healthy, exercise, and take naps if needed. I'm also more patient with my spouse and kids because I no longer worry about making ends meet. I feel blessed and abundant, and this attitude improves how I communicate with those around me. I'm also more charitable with my time, energy, and money. It makes me happy to see the relief and joy on other people's faces when offering a hand up instead of just a handout. I also feel a stronger connection with God and the universe. I spend more time praying and being in a state of gratitude. The money didn't make me a better person. I allowed myself to be my authentic self, instead of being stressed or dwelling on not having more."

Notice from the example above that you could experience all the transformative thoughts, feelings, and behaviors without having a million dollars. Again, because people focus so much on what's missing, they delay what they could have right now because of a belief that something else must happen first. "I'll be happy when..." Why not, "I'm choosing to be happy now because..."

STEP 2: CLEAR ALL NEGATIVE OR LIMITING BELIEFS

You have gained several exercises in the previous chapters for transforming worrisome thoughts into empowering affirmations. Of course, the fastest way to clear a fear-based belief is by asking two questions.

a) What am I afraid will happen if I try to reach this goal?

b) What would I rather believe instead, and what's one thing I can do to create the desired outcome?

Fear:

"I'm afraid it won't work out, and I'll be disappointed again."

Faith:

"I can get over being disappointed. Besides, not giving it my all would be a lot worse. I don't want to look back and regret not trying again. Therefore, I now choose to believe things are always working out for me if I keep learning and moving forward. I've got this!"

STEP 3: FEEL YOUR INTENTION ALREADY ACHIEVED

Positive emotion is the rocket fuel for your dreams. When you feel really good, you can accomplish anything. An obstacle gets in the way, a critic makes a demeaning remark, it starts raining outside, and you don't care because you're feeling passionate, joyful, calm, or even in love. Self-driven people have learned to master this step, which is why they are continually focused and motivated.

Once you've identified what you want, and cleared sabotaging beliefs, it's time to get yourself fired up for action. The best way to do so is by (1) implementing "feelization," and (2) doing your research. Sports psychologists train athletes to visualize their every move during competition. The goal is to imagine you are in the situation but moving in slow motion, making small adjustments that improve performance and results. Over time, high-performing athletes condition the muscles in their bodies to respond exactly how they imagine, so when in a competition, they don't have to think about what to do consciously. When athletes turn in an excellent performance, they often report not thinking about anything at the moment ("I was in the zone"). Their subconscious mind reverts to autopilot and allows them to produce a polished execution because the athlete trained their mind for success ahead of time.

Top sports psychologists began realizing, however, that not everyone is good at visualizing their performance. Plus, many athletes are kinesthetic and navigate through life by how they feel, rather than picturing things in their minds. Thus, these trainers began leading them through guided imagery sessions to "feel" their way through the experience. They will offer affirmations like, "Feel the strength and speed as you quickly spring off the line. Sense every muscle in your body firing in perfect unison as your body rotates through the air."

The second part of "feelization" entails flooding your body with winning emotions. "Imagine just scoring the game-winning goal, gazing up at the scoreboard, and confirming your victory. Feel the rush of excitement and the pleasure of all that hard work paying off. You are standing tall, full of energy. Full of life! You are a champion, and you feel so good, you might just take off into the air like Superman." Purposefully associating massive pleasure to training hard and achieving goals provides the extra boost of determination and resiliency needed to play at the highest levels in sports, business, and life. M. Scott Peck, the author of *The Road Less Traveled*, said it best: "Once you accept that life is difficult, it no longer feels that difficult." You embrace the struggle with enthusiasm, which transforms life's obstacles into challenges to gain wisdom from and triumph over! A top sports coach once told me, "In life, there are winners and learners. As long as you are doing one or the other, you will be successful on and off the field."

During one of our conversations, I shared these steps with Joe Vitale to get his take. Joe warmly smiled and said, "Tim, there is another part of this equation, and it's to do your research." I asked what he meant, and Joe replied, "How many times does someone say I want something, but never investigates what it would take to get it? If, for example, you want to manifest a dream car, have you looked online for the specific model, features, and color you desire? Or cut out a picture of it and made it the wallpaper on the home screen of your smartphone, so you see it all day long? Did you visit a dealership and take that car for a test drive? Have you calculated the monthly payments, including insurance and maintenance costs? Ever consider renting that car for a day? There are high-end rental companies who provide opportunities like this. Most importantly, are you imagining driving this car around town as you listen to the engine's purr and enjoy the feel of the luxurious leather seats?"

Joe's voice started sounding hypnotic. "What if your dream is to travel the world? Have you looked online to view travel packages for this? Where do you want to visit? What attractions do you want to see? Could you reach out to a travel agent for advice or read up on reviews from those who've already taken this trip? Have you created a vision board where you cut out pictures of the places or items you wish to see and glued them to a poster board that hangs near your desk or bed? Have you figured out how much the trip will cost, broken that price down into weekly payments, and automatically set up auto-withdrawal savings to automatically pull that amount into your "dream vacation" fund? Most would say no. They already decided it's out of reach, too expensive, or impossible on their salary. People shoot down their dreams before doing any kind of homework. Sure, it might be out of your price range right now, but you'd have the money if you saved for the next five or ten years."

As Joe spoke, my thoughts drifted to one of my dream goals: to make enough money as a professional keynote speaker that I didn't need to do anything else unless I wanted to. Inside, I felt that dream hadn't happened because I wasn't lucky enough to get my big break. Did you catch the self-limiting belief in that statement? *I'm not lucky enough.* Also, did I do my research? My answer was yes and no. I have pretty high standards for myself, so on the one hand, yes, I've done plenty of research. I've been role-modeling successful speakers, reading books on the subject, and putting the advice into action. It's led to my speaking numerous times on small and large stages across the country and in London, which was brilliant. Yet, there were many times where I'd only have six or seven keynotes in a year. But could I say that I put a full-time effort into being a full-time speaker? Honestly, I'd have to say no. I wasn't making prospecting calls every day. I wasn't reaching out to meeting planners or calling companies consistently. Almost every keynote I've provided came from someone calling me. I believe that occurred because I was doing the first couple of steps in this formula, but not all the steps, so I didn't attract everything I wanted.

As I continued thinking about Joe's remarks, I realized other subconscious conflicts and excuses had interfered with attaining this dream. First, I know a lot of professional speakers, and most of them are divorced. I'm sure there were other factors, but continuously being on the road is not good for a happy marriage. Plus, I've traveled plenty, and living in hotels and sitting for hours at airports sounds glamorous at first but gets old real quick. I've been with my wife for twenty-five years and plan on staying with her until the end. Sure, we've both plotted how to murder each other and get away with it. Yet, finding ways to stay in love, albeit hard work, is incredibly rewarding. You'll grow far more from that experience than from reading self-help books and attending seminars without your spouse. Plus, I love my two boys so much. I didn't want to miss any part of their childhood. Many older, wiser people told me children grow up so fast and to enjoy every minute of it, which I have.

I also found a way to make the same money as most well-paid motivational speakers by developing multiple income streams.

I spoke with a very successful motivational speaker one day who said he had fifteen high-paying gigs scheduled. When the financial market took a downturn, all the speaking contracts got canceled. He had no backup plan. No books, online programs, or coaching clients. Nada. One of the rules for creating financial abundance is never to put all your eggs into one basket. He used that hard-earned lesson to launch his first book and online program. I learned that lesson the hard way early on in my career and currently have six different ways to generate revenue, with keynote speaking being only one. Now that COVID-19 has swept across our planet, effectively canceling most public gatherings and keynotes for several months, I'm thankful for heeding the lessons of the past.

With all this new awareness gained from Joe, I took myself through the "Clearing" Experience in chapter nine to identify and clear sabotaging subconscious beliefs and employ synergy. Here's an abbreviated version of how it looked.

Dream: Full-Time Leadership Speaker

Pros:

- More fun travel
- Reach more people
- Higher potential income
- Greater social impact

Cons:

- A lot of time away from family
- Potential divorce
- Always on the road
- All eggs in one basket

- Having to do consistent "cold call" prospecting

Because there are more subconscious cons than pros, I didn't manifest that dream. Now that I am consciously aware of this, I can make a new decision, or adjust my goal. Here's what I decided:

Dream: Successful Leadership Trainer

Synergy:

- I publicly speak two or three times per month and can increase this if desired.
- I remain married and take my wife with me on the road since my kids are older now, so we can enjoy traveling together.
- I can reach just as many people, and even more, through social media.
- I still have multiple income streams through speaking, business consulting, executive coaching, private practice, books, and online programs.
- I've traded in "cold calling" for "new friend calling" and engage in this on a regularly scheduled basis.
- With COVID-19, I now provide more webinars and virtual training, while our brilliant researchers discover a vaccine.

With synergy, you end up with something more than you initially desired. Once you've completed those steps, it's time to unleash the power of your unconscious mind.

Step 4: Watch for Clues, Speedily Act upon Them as They Appear, and Adjust on the Fly

Once you are clear on what you want, have freed conflicting beliefs, and are emotionally charged for action, the rest of the process is exhilarating. Because you've done the hard work and taken the road less traveled, the universe will now reward you by sending the steps you need to get you to your goal. I refer to these steps as clues, and when they show up, act upon them with speed and enthusiasm.

Joe is so fond of the following quote that he turned it into a book with the same title: "Money loves speed!" In the book, Joe writes, "You must act on your intuitive impulses, and the opportunities that present themselves, and allow the results to manifest. The truth is there's no one way to achieve anything in this world. Some people get new cars by winning them, others by struggling to pay for them, others by happily paying for them, etc. You can't orchestrate the world to do your bidding. Instead, state your intentions and let the world arrange itself to bring your goals to you. You don't manufacture your outcomes. Instead, you participate in them by allowing your inner spirit to do most of the heavy lifting."

I asked Joe what he meant by that last sentiment about allowing your inner spirit to do most of the work. Joe replied, "Your unconscious mind is significantly more powerful than your conscious, analytical, pragmatic mind. Your conscious thinks about what's practical. Your unconscious believes anything is possible. You should trust in the power of your unconscious mind to find a way to make your dreams come true, rather than consciously struggling to figure out every step of the way."

"How do you get your unconscious mind to give you the steps?"

"Good question," he replied. "By following the first three steps of the manifesting formula in this book. Think of it like this. You ask God or the universe for a gift. Rather than just giving you the item or experience, God upgrades you by providing a treasure map that yields the gift and much more. Your job is to follow the treasure map clues, with each step bringing you closer to your desired outcome. Those who struggle are not clear about what they want or aren't taking action when the clues appear. Unfortunately, most don't recognize the clues or opportunities when they show up because skepticism clouds their ability to see them. Successful people are continually paying attention, taking action, and expecting miracles."

Successful people are continually paying attention, taking action, and expecting miracles!

"How do you know if something is a clue or if you're acting on the right opportunities?"

Joe replied, "It will feel right, logical, exciting, or fill you with inspiration. Inspiration means to be imbued with spirit. You won't always know if this step is the one that will take you across the finish line. Either it will, or it will take you to the next move in your journey. It reminds me of a classic tale told by Russell H. Conwell, founder and first president of Temple University. He wrote a book titled *Acres of Diamonds*. It tells the story of an African farmer who heard tales about other farmers who had made millions by discovering diamond mines. These tales so excited the farmer that he could hardly wait to sell his farm and go prospecting for diamonds himself. He sold the family farm and spent the rest of his life wandering the African continent, searching unsuccessfully for the gleaming gems that brought such high prices to the world's markets.

"The heart-wrenching part of the story is when the farmer learns that the farm he sold was sitting on a diamond mine. The moral is that what you seek isn't 'out there' in the world; it's right here at home. You must mine the opportunities that are currently within reach and follow the clues God is providing. When you go through one door, it unlocks the next one. There are no skipping doors. You cannot go from Door 1 to Door 12.

However, with proper education and coaching, you can learn to go through the doors quicker."

Joe's story made me think of a client who spoke of wanting to have extra spending money but felt stuck because she lived on a small retirement pension. I suggested she use this manifesting formula to attract additional funds, and the first couple of steps were to get clear on how much she wanted and believe this was possible. I asked how much extra spending money she desired, and she said, "I live modestly, so even if I only had a couple of hundred dollars a month, that would be wonderful." We then talked about creating value for others because it attracts abundance. At first, she shared that she couldn't think of any ways to add value since she was retired. I asked what she did in her profession, and she said she was an art teacher. She then went on to talk about how she loved painting. I asked if she had considered providing painting lessons, but this was no longer something she was interested in doing. I questioned if she had ever sold any of her paintings, and she said, "A couple of times, but that was many years ago." I recommended she start painting again since it provided so much pleasure, and to act on internal impulses or intuitions as they arose. At first, she was resistant but finally agreed to think about it.

About a week later, I received a telephone call. "Tim, you're never going to believe this! The day after our meeting, I felt the urge to look through my old painting supplies, so I acted on it, as you said. It felt good to hold the brushes and paints in my hands again. Over the next couple of days, I began painting a couple of red robins on small canvases. Then I decided to pull out a larger canvas and do a landscape painting. They take much more time, yet it feels so satisfying once the work is complete. It took a couple of days to complete this, but it was so much fun. I hadn't felt that good in a long time, so I decided to share my painting on Facebook. The next day an old friend of mine replied to the post and asked if I'd be willing to sell him the artwork. I was shocked! I replied, 'Sure, make me an offer.' He responded, 'How about two hundred dollars?'"

Step 5: Let Go and Be Needless!

The fifth step in manifesting anything is to develop a sense of being needless. That was a challenging concept for me to understand, so I reached out to Joe for clarification.

"I used to think being needless meant that you're not supposed to have wants or desires. I'd conjure up images of monks sitting in a Tibetan monastery all day chanting in meditation. I feel like this is a waste of potential. Life is about having a multitude of emotional experiences. Does anyone want to walk into an ice cream parlor that only offers vanilla? Some might say, 'So, you are okay with having bad things happen?' I'd reply, 'Sure. It's a normal part of life, and to resist it only prolongs the suffering. Besides, how do you know what happy is without sadness? How can you experience joy or appreciation without loss or scarcity? I'd prefer pleasurable experiences yet recognize the necessity of balance.'" I asked Joe what his thoughts were on the topic.

Joe sat back in his chair for a moment, played with a metal horseshoe that he had bent with his bare hands, and then replied, "I believe there are four steps human beings can travel through that lead to a genuinely fulfilling life. We start at victimhood and work our way to awakening by taking full responsibility for where we are in life. The third step is what I call Surrender, and it's what you are referring to as being needless. It's when we cultivate a feeling of abundance inside. It's an idea that we already have everything we need. So many of us have blessings beyond comparison. We have a warm home, a refrigerator that holds food, a car that we can drive, and a computer that we carry around in our pockets. Millions of people do not have those things that we take for granted."

Surrendering and being needless are states of mind where one recognizes that we are already whole, abundant, and blessed.

I felt a little embarrassed as Joe spoke. I remember my first cramped apartment that got so cold I'd light a dozen candles to stay warm on winter nights. But even then, I was grateful for having a place of my own. Now I live in a large home with a beautiful pool in the backyard. I'm richer than 95% of the population, and yet, if you heard some of the things I've thought to myself, you'd think I was still that broke kid from years ago. It's fascinating how our beliefs and the story we tell ourselves about our lives can twist reality.

"Joe, if I focus on attaining the things I want to manifest, am I focusing on what I don't currently have? Does that imply that there is a lack within me that would attract more scarcity? If so, should I let go of my desire for more things?"

Joe replied, "You can desire and pursue whatever you wish. The secret is to enjoy where you're at, and the pursuit of those goals. The founding fathers of America said everyone is entitled to the pursuit of happiness. I've sacrificed feeling happy at the moment because I was too busy being busy. I kept telling myself I'd be content when all these other things were satisfied, but then more things had to happen to be happy.

"There's an old story about a wealthy businessman who goes to a small fishing town for a much-needed vacation. He walks down to the seashore and sees a man in his mid-forties coming to shore with his boat. It appeared this fisherman had caught a lot of fish that day and was quite happy, as evidenced by the broad smile on his face. The businessman felt drawn to him, so he strolled down to the shore to say hello. The fisherman was friendly, and as the conversation lengthened, the businessman found his new friend loved his family, enjoyed his friends, was grateful for his work, and was quite successful at it.

"Feeling moved by the conversation, the businessman decided to offer advice for increasing the fisherman's assets. He said, 'You could grow a lucrative business here.' The fisherman asked how so. The businessman said, 'Well, you could start by investing in some other fishing boats and then hiring employees.'

"The fisherman said, 'Then what?'

"Growing more excited by the questions, the businessman said, 'Then you can put up a building here and set up a more extensive operation.'

"The fisherman replied, 'And then what?'

"The businessman continued, 'Then, over time, with a lot of hard work and energy, you will have quite a successful business with all these people working for you.'

"The fisherman asked, 'How long do you think all this would take?'

"The businessman thought for a second and replied, 'You're looking at about ten to fifteen years of hard work to accumulate the kind of capital that would set you up for life.'

"The fisherman patiently smiled and asked, 'If I worked in this way for ten or fifteen years, what would happen then?'

"The businessman smiled triumphantly and said, 'Well, then you could go on great vacations, spend more time with your family, do all the things you love, and get in some well-deserved fishing!'

"The fisherman paused for a moment to ponder the offer, and then replied, 'But that's what I'm doing right now.'"

Joe continued. "We somehow get it in our minds that we have to do all these things to be happy when it's our mindset that keeps us from feeling joyful. What if the goal isn't to be happy but to have a life full of meaning? People who feel like they have a sense of purpose always rate higher in life satisfaction. Even those who have made vast fortunes will often say that they felt unfulfilled and unsatisfied if they didn't have some goal to work toward."

"But Joe," I interjected, "What if you don't like where or how your life is right now? Are you supposed to just be happy and give up your ambitions?"

Joe looked at me compassionately and said, "The answer is no because giving up your dream doesn't create meaning or happiness. Instead, focus on cultivating an attitude of gratitude while going after things you desire. This way, you can enjoy the journey while chasing the destination. Otherwise, you might sabotage the very joy or happiness you seek because you believe the grass is greener on the other side when the grass can be greener where you stand if you water it with enough attention."

Focus on cultivating an attitude of gratitude while going after things you desire.

Once again, Joe was able to provide a practical answer to an existential question. Being needless doesn't mean pretending to be content if you aren't. Instead, it's more about acknowledging and appreciating the blessings you already have and setting purposeful goals that provide meaning and growth as you pursue them. I recalled a woman in her early sixties, Pam, who came to me because she wanted to eliminate her fear of flying. She related that she was preparing to take a cruise around the world but was nervous about the plane ride to Florida.

After further questioning, I realized that flying wasn't the real issue. Instead, it turned out Pam felt guilty about going on this trip. She said, "My husband and I had been saving money our whole lives for this fabulous retirement cruise. I wanted to take the vacation years earlier, yet my husband insisted it financially made more sense to go after he retired. He was a hard worker and very frugal with money. He never took a vacation, hardly ever splurged on us, and continuously put in long hours, even on the weekends, to save for retirement."

She continued. "I asked him many times throughout our marriage if we could have some fun now instead of waiting until we were older. But he refused, saying we had to be smart with our money and would have fun once we were debt-free. A week before my husband was supposed to retire, he had a heart attack and passed away." Then Pam looked me square in the eyes with a serious demeanor. "Tim, don't wait to go on vacation with your family. Take advantage of the time you have because we never know how many days we get."

Being needless doesn't mean pretending to be content if you aren't. Instead, it's about acknowledging and appreciating the blessings you already have and setting purposeful goals that provide meaning and growth as you pursue them.

Step 6: Live in the Moment with Gratitude

According to articles published through Harvard Medical School, those who enact this last step are far happier and emotionally healthier. One excerpt read, "Gratitude helps people feel more positive emotions, relish good experiences, improve their health, deal with adversity, and build strong relationships. People feel and express gratitude in multiple ways. They can apply it to the past (retrieving positive memories and being thankful for elements of childhood or past blessings), the present (not taking good fortune for granted as it comes), and the future (maintaining a hopeful and optimistic attitude)."

Living in the moment with gratitude allows your brain to generate the single emotion human beings tend to desire most: happiness. Gratitude also provides immediate gratification, which is something human beings also cherish. Yet, according to the research of Dr. Dan Gilbert, we do not find happiness outside ourselves. Instead, we synthesize it in our brains. Dan, the author of *Stumbling on Happiness,* challenges the idea that we'll be miserable if we don't get what we want. Our "psychological immune system" lets us feel happy even when things don't go as planned. Through his research, he found that most people come to terms with and accept situations that have happened when they believe they have no choice in the matter.

For example, if asked who would be happier in a year—a lottery winner or someone who became a wheelchair user—you'd think the answer is obvious. However, after interviewing people in those situations a year after the event occurred, the numbers revealed that both groups were equally happy. How can this be possible? Gilbert says it's because the pre-frontal lobes in the brain create "synthetic happiness." First, whatever happens, people adapt or get used to it. The highs of winning the lottery will eventually fade. So will the lows of being paralyzed if you continue living your life with purpose. When people are unable to change what's happened, the brain can cause you to believe the experience was "a good thing" because it might have prevented something worse from occurring, or it made you a better person. I often say the most painful experiences in my life contributed to becoming the person I am today.

At first glance, it may appear that effortlessly getting everything you want in life would lead to greater happiness, and some experiences are better than others. Granted, getting an ice cream sundae is better than receiving a punch in the nose. Yet, lots of ice cream sundaes can lead to Type 2 diabetes, and a punch in the nose could be just the wakeup call someone needs to better their life.

I once heard the late, great Zig Ziglar talk about a rancher who had some of his best horses escape through a broken fence. The rancher's neighbor was visiting and said, "Oh, this is bad!" The rancher replied, "How do you know?" The next day, those escaped horses returned and brought back beautiful wild mares with them. The neighbor saw this and said, "Oh, this is good!" The rancher replied, "How do you know?" That afternoon, the rancher's son tried taming one of the wild mares and broke his leg. The neighbor helped the rancher and his son, assessed the situation, and said, "Oh, this is bad." The rancher calmly looked at his son and said, "How do you know?" A week later, the cavalry visited the rancher to enlist his son, but he couldn't go on account of having a broken leg. The moral is not to jump to conclusions about what's good or bad. But instead, to patiently seek out the blessing in any situation.

Perhaps the most sweeping source of misery seems to arise from believing that situations are only good or bad. This all-or-nothing thinking robs the tranquility of one's mind because we either continually shame ourselves for past mistakes, make ourselves sick over missed opportunities, or relive injustices that keep one victimized in their mind. Dr. Gilbert's central message is that yes, we should have preferences that lead us in one direction versus another. Yet, when those preferences drive us too hard and too fast because we have over-rated the differences between these two futures, we are at risk. When our ambition is bounded, it leads us to work joyfully. When it is unbounded, it can lead us to lie, cheat, steal, hurt others, and sacrifice items of real value.

> ***"I am the happiest man alive. I have that in me that can convert poverty to riches, adversity to prosperity, and I am more invulnerable than Achilles; fortune hath not one place to hit me."***
> Sir Thomas Browne *Religio Medici* (1642)

Six Steps to Manifesting Anything

1. Identify and clarify what you want to manifest or attract into your life and why
2. Clear all negative (self-limiting) beliefs
3. Feel your intention already achieved
4. Do your research, watch for clues, speedily act upon them as they appear, and adjust on the fly
5. Let go and be needless
6. Live in the moment with gratitude

CHAPTER 12

FULFILLMENT NOW

"Occasionally in life there are those moments of unutterable fulfillment which cannot be completely explained by those symbols called words. Their meanings can only be articulated by the inaudible language of the heart."

Martin Luther King, Jr.

What if? Those two words often start a chain of worrisome thoughts that erase your ability to feel content in the present and hopeful about the future. However, if used appropriately, those two words could also unleash an entirely new set of possibilities and breakthroughs. For example, "What if there existed beliefs that just by choosing to have faith in them, would immediately unlock unlimited prosperity and fulfillment?" I decided to ask Joe if these beliefs existed and what they might be.

"Joe, are there any core beliefs that instantly produce a more fulfilling life?"

"Yes. One is that anything is possible. I don't know that there is anything that's impossible in the world. There may be, but what most consider impossible are only mental constructs. We look at reality and go, 'Well, that's not possible.' Yet, my experience has been people break improbable barriers all the time and continue doing so. Those who achieve, attain, and accomplish are continually expanding, learning, and growing because they believe in themselves and the power of the universe. If any life challenges are thrown at us, big or small, and we have the guiding principle that anything is possible, our mind is immediately going to look for solutions. If they exist, we'll find them. If they don't exist, we'll probably create them, all because of this fundamental belief. It merely serves us better than the alternatives like 'I'm stuck. I can't change things. That's how my family is. My doctor said this is the only outcome.' There are countless limiting beliefs out there that I don't want to entertain anymore. I want to come from a place of empowerment."

Those who achieve, attain, and accomplish are continually expanding, learning, and growing because they believe in themselves and the power of the universe.

Joe continued. "Another belief I have found useful is, 'I deserve good things, happiness, love, and success.' Too many of us have an unconscious belief that we're not good enough. We're not likable or lovable in some form or another. Like we're falling short of some sort of ideal that we have in our mind. We need to start appreciating ourselves and building up our self-worth through realizing we became worthy of love the day we were born. We don't need to be better or have more stuff to deserve love. We are already enough. We're already inherently good, and our life is a gift from the universe. This isn't an ego trip. I'm talking about self-appreciation. It's not bloating ourselves up to appreciate that we are kings and queens of our own lives.

"Believing anything is possible, you are already enough, and you deserve good things are powerful bottom-line operating beliefs. If we have those in our bag of tricks and start moving forward in life, we're going to get better results. We're going to be happier, healthier, and more optimistic. Instead of rolling over and playing dead or giving up when things get tough, you'll be able to stand on your own two feet and know that things are going to work out for you in one way or another."

We need to start appreciating ourselves and building up our self-worth through realizing we became worthy of love the day we were born.

I found myself enthusiastically nodding in agreement. "I wholeheartedly agree, Joe! Those beliefs cause your brain to pay attention to the clues for how to triumph in any situation. It's skepticism or a lack of faith that prevents people from activating their full potential. The fear of being let down or getting hurt causes one to dwell on why things won't work out, rather than focusing on how they could."

I decided to play devil's advocate and channel the thoughts of a critic to see how Joe would respond. "Dr. Vitale, you say anything is possible. Can a man give birth? What if I'm three feet tall, fifty years old, and want to be a starting player in the NBA. How do I manifest that?"

Joe grinned as though he had heard these questions many times before. Then he asked, "Did you know male seahorses are the ones who get pregnant? The female deposits her eggs inside the male's pouch, and he fertilizes the eggs inside the pouch. Instead of growing their baby seahorses inside a uterus as human moms do, seahorse dads carry their babies in a pouch that provides oxygen and nutrients. Depending on the species, male seahorses typically carry the eggs for two to four weeks and give birth to between 100 and 1,000 babies through muscular contractions. Human mothers are God's greatest creations. Yet, I believe if humankind needed men to deliver babies, they could model seahorses."

I sat back in wonder. I didn't know seahorses did that. I looked it up, and a woman whose pen name is Ocean Allison wrote about it. Fascinating!

"What about playing in the NBA?" I asked.

Joe replied, "Is your goal really to play in the NBA? Or is your real intention to prove these principles false? I'm saying you can improve your quality of life by applying the same success principles that have empowered so many others. When someone criticizes this idea, they are revealing their own limiting beliefs. Keep in mind, you get to keep the beliefs you argue for and defend. Do you really want to fight for ideas that hold you back?"

You get to keep the beliefs you argue for and defend. Do you really want to fight for ideas that hold you back?

I thought that was a rational response to a cynical question. "Makes sense, Joe. If you spend your energy focusing only on why things won't work, all you'll end up producing is that outcome." I continued with my questioning. "Joe, in your book *The Attractor Factor,* you used the term 'chasing ghosts' to describe how people pursue desires they believe provide fulfillment. Yet, it's often not the goal attainment, but what we think achieving that goal will do for us that's most attractive. Can you elaborate on this?"

Joe picked up a pencil from his desk and presented it to me. "Tim, one of my favorite exercises is to grab a pencil and paper and then write down what I want. Next, I jot down what I think will happen once I've reached this goal. What will this do for me? Then I write down anything that might interfere with my attaining this desire. I continue scribbling answers to both of those questions until I've unburied my real aspirations and beliefs about what's possible. The great thing about a pencil is that it has lead at one end and an eraser on the other. At any point in the exercise, I can erase limiting fears that arise and replace them with more empowering viewpoints."

Joe's pencil exercise is powerful because of how the questions excavate subconscious beliefs that need to be updated before taking action toward whatever goal you have. You'll have a chance to participate in this exercise at the end of the chapter.

Still playing the role of a skeptic, I asked Joe, "How do you respond when people say it's easy for you to give all this advice about letting go and being needless since you're already rich?"

Joe reflected for a moment and then replied, "I became wealthy as a result of applying these principles. Remember, I started out homeless. Let's look at why people continually find reasons for why things won't work out. The brain is wired for survival. Our reticular activating system, for example, is preset to keep you alive, and we want it that way. It's always scanning our environment for threats. Some studies suggest there's around fourteen billion bits of information at any one second that your brain has to examine to ensure your safety. Is there a car coming at me? Is there a psychological or emotional threat coming from the outside world?

"It assesses the situation in a nanosecond and determines what should be done to protect you without checking for conscious approval based on your pre-wired instincts and ingrained subjective beliefs. Thus, finding evidence for why something won't work is simply a form of self-protection. Skeptics don't want to do something that could be a threat to their survival or self-image. Their default system for self-preservation is working very well. Yet, you can train your mind to do much more than just survive. You can teach it to achieve your goals, attract the love of your life, increase wealth, or have a spiritual awakening. Sure, you can use your mind power to seek evidence that seems to prove these statements false. But all you'll end up doing is blocking yourself from what you could experience if you had more faith and a little less fear.

"The world is an optical illusion. You can look out there and see whatever you want. If you are coming from a critical, victimhood standpoint, you'll find plenty of evidence that the world is scary or out to get you. People want to prove what they already believe is true because we like to be right, even if being right keeps us unhappy. Making yourself feel powerless also saves you from having to make difficult choices, which psychologically can feel comforting.

"Of course, all of this is happening unconsciously. Few would admit to consciously selecting victimhood. It's undoubtedly strange if you've had a critical mindset to suddenly adopt this attitude that you are responsible for everything you experience in life and that anything is possible. However, like anything else that's new, it feels awkward at first, but gradually you become more comfortable with your new reality."

You can train your mind to do much more than just survive. You can teach it to achieve your goals, attract the love of your life, increase wealth, or have a spiritual awakening.

"Not only comfortable but ecstatic," I said. "I'm sure you've seen this too, Joe. My clients often start out skeptical but hopeful that we will produce the results I suggest. When their goals are attained, they fill with jubilation and surprise. I'll hear comments like, 'I still can't believe this has happened,' or 'I'm shocked that it was so easy! How is that possible?' I tell them you always have a choice. You can operate from fear or faith. Fear causes you to feel sad, sick, angry, frustrated, and depressed because the subconscious belief is, *I can't do anything to improve my situation.* Faith comes from supporting the opposite perspective. *I have the power to improve my life.*

Joe nodded. "It seems so obvious when you say that, Tim, but we both know that there are many out there who disagree. What they're doing is arguing for their own limitations. Is the answer to give up and live a life of quiet desperation, as Henry David Thoreau said? Aren't you interested in an alternative? Many are not because they feel in some shape or form, they're just going to get hurt or be disappointed. But this disempowering thinking needs a reality check. True, not everything is going to work out, and there are times where you will be hurt or disappointed.

Even when fully applying the Law of Attraction, there are going to be bumps in the road. There will always be rainy days, times when you catch a cold, or when someone doesn't follow through on a promise. Faith isn't about living on Easy Street. It's about holding onto your beliefs when things are going the opposite of how you want them to be."

Faith isn't about living on Easy Street. It's about holding onto your beliefs when things are going the opposite of how you want them to be.

Joe leaned back in his chair again and smiled. "There's a hit TV show called *Downton Abbey,* and the writers for it are absolutely genius. I watched one episode and was addicted to the whole thing. There's a scene where a woman lost her husband in a car accident and was devastated. She's crying and shaking as she confides in her friend, 'I'm afraid to love again. I'm so scared I'll be hurt.' How her friend replies gave me chills. 'You will be afraid, and you will get hurt. But you must love again.' We are all going to get knocked to our knees at times. Yet, we must get back up because life has a balance, and there are days filled with joy just ahead. That's the reality check for when life seems to be strangling your soul.

"I'm currently going through some gut-wrenching experiences that are, at times, excruciatingly painful. People might think, 'Joe, you're the Law of Attraction guru. Why are you manifesting these painful experiences into your life?' My answer is, 'Because I'm human and still have more growing to do.' What's getting me through is the reality that there'll be another day with sunshine. There'll be another day where things work out really well. I remind myself that I'll be okay. I'll get through this and come out on the other side better than before."

We are all going to get knocked to our knees at times. Yet, we must get back up because life has a balance, and there are days filled with joy just ahead.

I agree with Joe's sentiments about life being in balance. No matter how dark it gets at night, morning always arrives. No matter how harsh the winter, summer shows up every year.

Skeptics may say, "What about in Alaska? It's dark six months in a row." True, but then it's followed by six months of straight daylight. Everyone wants life to be easy, but where's the challenge in that? What would force you to grow? Why is climbing a mountain more extraordinary than a hill? Because it's harder to do.

Buddha once said that life is suffering, but when you recognize this, you are no longer afraid of it, which reduces the extent of it. How would you discover what you're truly capable of accomplishing without adversity? This doesn't mean you have to like what happens. In fact, I despise many of the hateful things human beings do to one another. Yet, pain is unavoidable. Emotional intelligence and mental toughness are about learning how to move through the pain with grace. Yes, this is easier said than done, but it's something worth striving for. It's also the only constructive way I'm aware of that helps people put the pieces of their hearts back together after trauma and tragedy occur.

Emotional intelligence and mental toughness are about learning how to move through the pain with grace.

"Joe, there is controversy over the idea of taking ownership of everything in your life. You've said before that at an unconscious level, we attract everything in our lives. If that's the case, are you suggesting those who lose children to cancer or experience sexual abuse manifested that?"

Joe slowly nodded. "That is an important question, Tim. Allow me to explain. I believe we have the opportunity to travel through four phases of personal and spiritual development.

"Most start at level one, which is victimhood. Whether by our own doing or not, we have experienced mental, physical, emotional, sexual, or spiritual hardships. The motto of victimhood is, 'I'm broken, and there's nothing I can do about it.'

"The second level is empowerment. At this stage, we begin taking responsibility for our thoughts, feelings, and behaviors. We also start releasing ourselves from wounds of the past. The motto is, 'I am already whole and can choose my beliefs and destiny.' At this stage, we decide to take full responsibility, which means the ability to respond to everything experienced in life. Saying that a person attracted sexual abuse or the loss of a child in this framework is not done to blame the victim. Instead, it's a way to reclaim your emotional freedom. Your soul may have chosen this path before you were born, so you could experience the more profound healing and spiritual growth that come from forgiveness and resolution. Perhaps your painful experiences were necessary for you to become the person you were born to be. My pain of being homeless provided the spiritual and psychological hunger I needed to become the person I am today."

Saying that a person attracted sexual abuse or the loss of a child in this framework is not done to blame the victim. Instead, it's a way to reclaim your emotional freedom.

Many, including myself, have experienced physical, verbal, or sexual abuse in childhood. Now that it's happened, what are we going to do with it? Joe's approach provides the path out of victimhood and into empowerment. I wondered what steps came after that, so I asked Joe, "What are the other two phases of psychological and spiritual development?"

"The third level is surrender, and it's where we begin releasing outdated ideas that certain expectations must occur to feel happy, content, or prosperous. We also release the belief that future material desires must be attained to feel fulfilled. The motto is, 'I accept full responsibility for my life and am at peace with who I am.'

"Awakening is the fourth phase, and it occurs when you are fully alive and present now, rather than being consumed with the past or future. Realizing nothing is missing, and life is unfolding as it's supposed to, you find yourself in a joyful dance with the universe. The motto is, 'It's all good.'"

Joe's brief explanation of the fourth phase reminded me of the impatient student who kept asking his teacher to help him become enlightened. His teacher replied, "Can you hear the birds singing joyfully in the distance?"

"Yes, teacher, but I want to be enlightened."

The teacher said, "Yes, but can you feel the cool breeze pressing against your skin?"

"Yes, but I desire enlightenment, teacher."

The teacher continued through the day, chopping wood and carrying water, all with a smile on his face. Later, the frustrated student asked again, "Teacher, when will you reveal the secrets to being enlightened?"

His teacher patiently replied, "Will you pause to take in the wonder of the setting sun this evening?"

Confused, the student responded, "Teacher, what does a sunset have to do with enlightenment?"

The teacher answered, "Enlightenment isn't a place or goal. It's a state of mind and open-ended gratitude for the magic and wonders that are continually occurring around you. It's feeling awe and appreciation for the sights, sounds, and sensations that others do not notice because of their busy minds."

The student thought about how he had dismissed the singing of the birds, the refreshing breeze on his sweaty brow, and how magnificent the sunset is over the mountainside. "Teacher, what happened when you experienced enlightenment?"

The teacher smiled broadly once more. "Before I was awakened, I chopped wood and carried water. After I awakened, I chopped wood and carried water. Yet, I suddenly found tremendous satisfaction in doing both."

Enlightenment isn't a place or goal. It's a state of mind and open-ended gratitude for the magic and wonders that are continually occurring around you. It's feeling awe and appreciation for the sights, sounds, and sensations that others do not notice because of their busy minds.

Six Keys to Unlocking Fulfillment

I knew Joe subscribed to intentionally causing a sense of fulfillment in the present based upon the books he's written. I asked if he had any specific suggestions for unlocking inner peace right now, regardless of what you've been through in the past. He said there are six keys, or principles, that lead to a more fulfilling life.

1. **Take total responsibility for your experiences.** That doesn't mean you caused them, but on some level, you attracted them. You are responsible for them. That's not good or bad. Simply use the experiences to learn about yourself. Get clear and choose what you prefer to experience.

2. **You are absorbing beliefs from the culture itself.** If you are watching violent movies or regularly viewing "Breaking News" video clips on your smartphone, you're filling your mind with the very vibe that will attract more of what you are absorbing. Violence invites more aggression and fear. Mother Teresa said she would never attend an antiwar rally because it contains the same

energy that creates more war. Choose your surroundings carefully.

3. **You are not the ruler of the earth, but you are the ruler of your thoughts.** You have tremendous power and can move mountains with the right ideas and actions. Allow the divine within you to rule over your human ego and strive for balance in all things.
4. **You can change your thoughts.** This often feels impossible to believe because it's not typical for most people. But what you think is mostly based on old ideas and habits. Pay attention to your thoughts all day long. If you don't like your course of thinking, consciously redirect it by selecting new thoughts.
5. **You can do the impossible.** What you believe to be the restraints of time and space right now may simply be the limits of our current understanding. No one knows what is impossible. If you are inclined to try something new and different, then so be it. Go for it. Make it so. You may be creating a path never seen before. Dare something worthy.
6. **Whatever image you add feeling to long enough will eventually manifest.** If you fear something or love something, you are adding energy to it. Anything you fear or love will tend to be attracted into your life. Choose your passions wisely.

"Joe, these keys are full of wisdom, but the first one is still difficult for most to comprehend. Can you elaborate on it a little more?"

Joe replied, "Tim, nobody wants 'bad things' to show up. We aren't consciously asking for rain on the day of our big parade. Nobody wants a drought either. It all comes back to how you deal with it. How do you want to approach these situations? You are going to have conditions that—and these are subjective terms—are peaceful and painful. So how do you want to go through them? I think that's the message you and I keep talking about. Do you want to go through this world with an internal sense of control, adjusting how you're looking at things so that you can modify your level of suffering and fulfillment? Or travel through life feeling like you have no control over anything, and you're at the mercy of a cold, uncaring world?

"This is about consciously deciding to show up and answering how you want to live your life. That means looking at what's really driving you and being more self-aware and accountable. You've got to own the situation so you can do something with it or use it to your advantage. Responsibility gives you the ability to respond. It doesn't mean it's your fault that bad things have happened. Instead, it's about taking your power back when they do."

Do you want to go through this world with an internal sense of control, adjusting how you're looking at things so that you can modify your level of suffering and fulfillment? Or travel through life feeling like you have no control over anything, and you're at the mercy of a cold, uncaring world?

Joe continued. "Also remember, you're not attracting things you are consciously thinking about. You're attracting into your life what you unconsciously believe with emotion. Your unconscious mind has been preprogrammed, usually not by you, through the information you downloaded from your parents, friends, community, religion, culture, and society. You absorbed all of that. So, by the time you're eight years old, you're pre-wired like a robot. When you get to be an adult, you're wondering why you attract this particular stuff into your life. But you're not doing it consciously. You're doing it unconsciously, which is why we focus so much on your unconscious programming. I don't wake up in the morning thinking, 'Boy, I hope some problems show up so I can grow today!' I don't want problems any more than you do. However, I do expect that challenges will arise and am convinced I'll be able to handle them without the need to be crippled by stress.

"My father died a few months ago, and I'm currently going through a long-term divorce. I'm also caring for a woman who's developed four different brain diseases and has been near death for six months. I'm dealing with the grief of my dad, the loss of a twenty-year marriage, and a friend who has been barely hanging on. Every day I get up thinking, *How do I get through this?* Some days are easier than others, but when life has brought you to your knees, little slogans like 'face your fears,' 'look for the silver lining,' and 'just do it' don't seem to mean much. That's why you've got to take a deep-dive into your unconscious mind and find out what beliefs might draw you to events like this so you can make sense of it and live your life with meaning and purpose. Andres, the billionaire I told you about earlier, told me that he expects problems every day. In fact, he said he liked them. 'It's like playing chess. There's the problem that shows up. Now I need to make a move to see what to do about it.' He re-shifted my perception of problems."

**It's like playing chess.
There's the problem that shows up.
Now I need to make a move to see
what to do about it.**

"Joe, as I listen to you, I feel empathy for what you're going through. I even have the urge to say I'm sorry you're going through these things. Yet, after pondering the six keys you shared, perhaps feeling sorry isn't the best response. Instead, perhaps I should feel grateful and amazed that you can recognize all these human experiences are there to help you grow. If you have these issues, it's because you attracted them to you. This is not blaming; it's empowering. Shakespeare said the world is your stage, and we are all characters in your play. I think the world is homeostatic and desires balance. If we get too down, life will find a way of bringing us back up. And if we get too high, life will put us in check to keep us humble."

Joe nodded. "Yes, Tim, I believe that life does prune us. I've been married twice. The first marriage lasted twenty years, and so did the second. Now, I'm thinking about a third marriage. You asked earlier why the expert in teaching the Law of Attraction would attract this? Well, let's look at that.

"I've said many times that you've got to be ruthlessly honest with yourself and get to the heart of what's most important to you. When I finally got honest with myself, I realized I wasn't happy in my first marriage and wasn't admitting it. So, the universe decided to give me a reality check."

I jumped in. "Joe, I've had those reality checks as well. I recall working at a psychiatric inpatient facility around the age of twenty-two. It was a dangerous place, and I hated working there. Yet, I didn't want to quit just because it was a hard job. One day, I was brought into the administrator's office and was accused of stealing one of the patient's clothes. I was hurt and angry because that accusation was ridiculous. The real issue was how poorly many of the psych nurses were treating the patients, and I spoke up about it. That's what got me terminated. I was so upset for a couple of days. But then I realized I got what I wanted. I didn't have to work there anymore, and I didn't have to quit either. Life granted my wish. It wasn't how I would have planned it, but the result was the same, and I'm glad I got out of there when I did. Shortly after, the whole hospital was closed down."

You've got to be ruthlessly honest with yourself and get to the heart of what's most important to you.

"Yes," said Joe. "Life does provide what you subconsciously request, but not always in the way you want it. The second thing I had to get clear on was my own philosophy of life. How am I going to live my life? While going through the divorce, I leased a house that had a plaque hanging on the wall. It read, *No longer argue about what a good man is. Be one.—Marcus Aurelius.* The universe is always sending you messages. Another one of his statements is, 'If it's endurable, endure it and stop complaining.' Those two sentiments really carried me through over the following eight months. I remember walking the streets at night just talking to God and wondering how I had gotten to this point. As I'm strolling along, this thought pops into my mind. *Is this endurable? It is awful, but is it endurable? It is pitiful, but is it endurable? This hurts like hell, but is it endurable? Yes, yes, and yes. Then endure it!*

Joe reminded me of a college history professor as he continued. "Stoicism, which was popular during the time of Marcus Aurelius, has a very stark way of viewing reality. It looks at objective reality and does its best to eliminate emotions that could take away from the moment. I'm sure Marcus and the gang from the Stoic times of centuries ago knew nothing about the Law of Attraction. They lived in a world where emperors would kill every tenth person just to make a point. You didn't know from one day to the next if you were going to be number ten. This was a time that was hard to survive in, let alone trying to thrive in.

"But then I started wondering, *What if the Law of Attraction merged with Stoicism in some way?* What if you have the objective reality of where you are in your life and also the knowledge that you can create a new reality? If you use specific principles and pay attention to how the brain works, while also incorporating vision boards, affirmations, etc., you can become far stronger by applying both philosophies. Then it struck me. I wouldn't even be entertaining this new realm of possibility if I hadn't been thrown into the nightmare of divorce and found that plaque hanging on a random wall of a leased home.

"Tim, I've heard you use the metaphor of having your head in the clouds but also your feet on the ground. That's what it feels like when you are both a part of heaven and Earth at the same time. You're being practical and using the full power of your pre-frontal lobes at the same time to maximize your potential. Having the ability to think, *How do I want to approach this situation?* instead of feeling victimized by it is powerful. I love that."

"FULFILLMENT" EXPERIENCE

Grab a pencil and paper and write as many answers as you can for the following questions.

What do I want to accomplish?

What will attaining this do for me?

What might interfere with my attaining this goal?

What would I rather believe instead?

How do I want to approach this situation moving forward?

"No longer argue about what a good man is. Be one!"
"If it's endurable, endure it, and stop complaining."
Marcus Aurelius

CHAPTER 13

FEAR TO FAITH

"A life of fulfillment comes from within; through the knowledge that you were created with everything, you need to be happy."

Deepak Chopra, author of *The 7 Spiritual Laws of Success*

A question frequently asked when first learning how to take charge of your thoughts is, "How long do I have to keep doing this until it works?" I reply, "How long do you have to guide the steering wheel while driving before the car can drive itself?" You can upgrade a limiting belief or break a bad habit rather quickly, and it doesn't require much reinforcement. However, your conscious thinking needs continual monitoring and adjusting. Your brain is an amazing, complex organ, and it, like a steering wheel, must be guided for you to reach your desired destinations. That means you'll need to monitor your thoughts and beliefs for the duration of your life. The good news is that it gets much easier because you are now paying attention to how your thinking influences you from moment-to-moment. This conscious state of mind is referred to as mindfulness in today's culture.

The tools in this book will significantly enhance your quality of life now and in the future—if you use them. Yet, true fulfillment comes from continuously paying attention to, and improving your unconscious beliefs, since these hidden viewpoints fuel what you consciously think about all day long.

As we reach the end of this journey together, I encourage you to make it one of your most important missions in life to equip yourself with an empowering set of beliefs. Life will provide plenty of opportunities for you to pause, go within, and decipher how your subconscious perspectives influence the decisions you're making. You can also use your current situation as feedback for how your mind is already programmed. If there is something you don't like about your confidence, finances, relationships, health, or surroundings, it's a signal that you must enhance the beliefs that attract or perpetuate these experiences. I used to get frustrated by this, thinking, *Why do I always have to be the one to make things better?* The answer is, "Because you are the one with the awareness and power to do so. It's your life. Be responsible for it."

If there is something you don't like about your confidence, finances, relationships, health, or surroundings, it's a signal that you must enhance the beliefs that attract or perpetuate these experiences.

I want to share with you one more personal conversation with Joe about one of my deepest fears. My hope is that it will encourage you to face your biggest insecurities head-on so you can triumph over them.

I was working on my own beliefs as I wrote the early chapters of this book. One of my struggling points was when I thought about just going for whatever I wanted without worrying about how much money it would cost. Most people have deep-seated issues with money. I certainly did. We've been programmed, especially in the United States, to worship money, and if you ask the average American if they have enough of it, they'd reply, "There's never enough."

I'd think about the belief that held me back and where it came from, but I still wasn't sure. I felt like my family was financially secure, growing up. My dad put in many doubles and overtime at the steel mill where he worked, and he did a fantastic job of providing for us. Of course, there were tough times like when he almost died at work when I was twelve years old. But even then, I was lucky enough to have grandparents who helped take care of us. Growing up, I never felt like I had a lot of money, and when I got out on my own, I never felt like I could just buy whatever I wanted. I was in a never-ending cycle of always just getting by. I lived on a tight budget in my twenties and thirties, worrying about how I would pay the bills each month. Even when I started making more money, my expenses also increased, and I'd still feel broke, just at a higher level.

But this didn't seem to be the root of my fear. Realizing these things didn't ease the sick feeling in my stomach. I wasn't sure what the belief that drove that feeling was, so I started asking myself this question repeatedly: "What's the worst thing that could happen?" After conjuring up several worst-case scenarios, I landed upon something that seemed to resonate in my gut. "I can't relax around money because I might run out of it." That seemed to be the core fear driving all the other ones.

Of course, the coach in me instantly asked, "And then what?" Sometimes you have to take the worry and play it out to the end before realizing you'd still be okay if the worst happened. I thought, *Would my wife and kids abandon me if I couldn't keep up with the mortgage or car payments? No. They wouldn't be happy about selling their home, but we are a close family, and they'd be supportive and encouraging.*

"If we lost all our money, we'd be homeless." *Nope. We could move in with our friends or my in-laws until I realized how to get back on my feet financially.*

Through this round of Q&A with myself, another core belief surfaced that made me feel good. *I always land on my feet. I'm too resourceful and relentless for things to ever get that far out of hand. Plus, I've never actually run out of money. Not once. I've always found my way, and God stepped in and provided a miracle in my life when I couldn't.* These comforting realizations came pouring into my mind because I've kept my hands firmly on my brain's steering wheel for years.

I had identified the fear that held me back from playing more prominently in life. I took the limiting belief through the "Clearing" Experience but still felt tight inside. I justified this by thinking the new perspective hadn't completely taken hold yet, and to give it time. Time passed, and I still felt unsettled, so I asked my unconscious to provide me with the real issue and to heal it. A couple of hours later, I was watering flowers in the backyard, and an idea flooded into my mind: *If I ran out of money, I would feel humiliated.* Suddenly, a flash of different memories poured through my imagination—memories of being bullied and feeling so angry with myself for being scared. My body would freeze, and I wouldn't be able to do anything but shake or cry. I stood up to one of the bullies in sixth grade, which was frightening for me. As we started wrestling on the ground, he sat on me and held my arms down. He was twice my size, and I couldn't do anything but yell at him to get off me. Ironically, he didn't do anything but hold me down, yet my brain was freaking out, and I felt humiliated.

Often, I say it's not the experiences you go through, but the beliefs that come from them that determines your quality of life. The notion that formed in my unconscious was whether I fight back or not, I'm still going to lose and be humiliated. That's a pretty awful viewpoint to have. Yet, I had so many memories of trying to stand up for myself, which felt good and bad at the same time. One bully, who targeted me throughout high school, pushed me so much that I had no other choice but to fight back. It was during a dance in my senior year that I finally physically defended myself. I won that fight and almost got kicked out of school because of it. Afterward, teachers treated me like I was the bully. Even worse, now every other bully in the school wanted to see how tough I was, which was horrible. I have accepted the fact that I am a healer, not a fighter. But it still felt humiliating and paralyzing. *No matter what I do, I can't win.* Finally, I had figured out my deepest, darkest fear.

I took myself through the "Forgiveness" Experience and placed my inner child in the chair on the glass's other side. Of course, I removed the glass wall immediately and started the process by hugging him. After going through this, I felt a wave of peace flow through me. The next day, I was driving to the office, and my wife called. She said, "I think that maybe for our son's sixteenth birthday in December we could go on a Disney vacation." Usually, my first response would be, "Let me take a look at the finances." However, after clearing the old fear of being humiliated and realizing that I live in an abundant world that always provides for me, I replied, "Let's do it!" Her response was, "I'm sorry. I was trying to get a hold of my husband." She was delighted, and so was I. We went on that trip and had the best time ever. Unfortunately, Disney World closed a few months later due to the Coronavirus, and when it reopens, it won't be the same experience again for a long time. I'm so thankful we went. My family will have those special memories of our son's sixteenth birthday our whole lives, and we got to experience the new *Star Wars* attractions pre-COVID-19. It would have been horrible if I had said no to the trip because of experiences from thirty-five years ago!

I love synchronicity. When you start moving toward your intentions, the universe begins moving your goals toward you as well. I wanted to share the experience I just told you about with Joe, so I called him and recounted the story. "Isn't that weird how my wife would ask me to get out of my comfort zone immediately after shifting that old belief?"

"It's actually not weird," replied Joe. "It's the way the world works because we're all connected. We're all one, and she's more energetically connected to you because you're living with her. You've demonstrated a few things. One is you became aware of the belief. You were struggling with an issue and perhaps had thought of it before, but this time there was a light on it, and you were able to think, *Oh, that's the limiting belief.* Then—and this is the thing that's so wonderful about beliefs—sometimes just looking at it weakens it. Bringing it into the light is the first step toward dissolving it. A belief is just a thought that we subconsciously fill with energy. You kept repeatedly feeding that viewpoint, albeit unconsciously, but now you inspected it and thought, *Wait a minute. Is this authentic?*

"Does anybody ever really run out of money? I mean, there's always money in some way, shape, or form. Over those ten years, when I was living in poverty, I thought, *I'm not going to have enough money.* Yet, somehow those bills got paid during that time. Miraculously, the money showed up and kept showing up, so that's the first thing. You became aware of it, then released it, and wanted to replace it with a new idea. However, when you install a new belief, it doesn't always feel comfortable right away. You're doing something you haven't done before, and that can feel unsettling at first. Once we make a decision, a ripple effect travels through our body and mind and into the universe. In some metaphysical, esoteric, or quantum physics way, it ripples out into the world like tossing a pebble into a pond. Who does it reach first? The people who are most directly impacted by that decision. For you, it was your wife. You shifted your energy, and the universe responded accordingly. Suddenly, your wife has an impulse to call you and ask for what she wants, and bam, both of your desires are satisfied."

Joe sat back and smiled like a kid who has a secret. "To the rest of the world, it's a fluke. It has no meaning whatsoever. Yet, to those awakened, it carries a profound message. What you just shared is a step-by-step process for anybody, no matter what his or her issue. Look for the operating belief, shine a light on it, question it, and ask what you'd rather believe instead. You also asked the universe, 'Is it okay for me to go on this trip?' It replied, 'Yes! Do it now because you don't know what's coming down the pike in a few months.'

"After my divorce, I began a new relationship, and we kicked around the idea of taking a wonderful trip to Italy. I started hanging pictures of Italy on the wall and putting my vision board together, figuring we'd go one day. A week later, I woke up one morning, looked at the vision board, and thought, *You know, we should just go. What are we doing looking at the wall? We should just go.* Then I started looking up flights, villas, and other things for our trip. We decided to stay for thirty days and had a lot of fun making up the itinerary. Then one morning, I had another idea. *Somebody should pay for this other than me.*

"None of this thinking would have been there if I hadn't created the vision board or decided to act. Now I'm upping the game by getting somebody else to finance the trip. I remembered that there was a translator in Italy who was a fan of my work, so I contacted him and said we were coming to Italy. I then suggested he put on an event there to help pay for the expenses, and I'd give him his fair share. Long story short, he put on four seminars with the one in Milan having four hundred people in attendance. It entirely paid for the trip, and we traveled first class. That's possible for all of us if you believe it is, and don't put limitations on God, the universe, or yourself. Remember, I was homeless at one time. I was in poverty. If I can change, anyone can. Andres was also homeless, struggling, and starving in Thailand. Now he's a captain of industry because he changed his beliefs. There are plenty of stories about people who have been far worse off than those reading this book. The ability to change is clearly possible for all of us."

The ability to change is clearly possible for all of us.

"Joe, to be honest, I stopped putting up vision boards many years ago because I got tired of the boards' goals not coming true. It made me feel like I wasn't as smart, talented, or lucky as those success stories you're referring to."

Joe nodded in recognition. "Tim, those were the beliefs that I had at one time too. That's why I wasn't taking action in the way that I could have been. It's very easy to start blaming or go into self-pity. But when you're accountable, you think, *My experience is this way only because of the beliefs in my mind, and I can change this right now.* That is much more empowering than holding back because you're afraid of feeling like a fraud or not being good enough."

I felt better for admitting my fears and hearing Joe's reply. I then said, "Joe, your perspective strengthens people. You're saying, look, it's not that God doesn't like me, or the universe is karmically trying to beat me up. Instead, it's my unconscious beliefs that held me back, and I can improve this immediately by applying the experiences I've acquired through reading this book. That gives us power. Instead of fighting and resisting problems, we can embrace the challenges and excel in ways that once felt impossible."

Joe smiled broadly. "Exactly! I believe that life is all about awakening, and there's an art to cultivating our inherent power. As I've said before, there are four phases of awakening. The first is a state of victimhood. It's a lower consciousness where most of the beliefs center on blaming other people, shirking responsibility, and making excuses. We've all been there, and sometimes we still visit this stage because it's easy to point fingers. Most people in victimhood will probably disagree with this, which is a sign they are in it.

"The second phase is much more fun. It's empowerment, and we enter it often through reading self-help books or working with a coach. It's a new level of awareness like, *Wow, I didn't even think I was behaving this way, or that my beliefs might've been holding me back, but I can see how they were now.* This insight moves you in a more empowered direction, and you feel like Superman or Superwoman. It instantly feels like anything is possible.

"But then there's the third phase, and that's what I call Surrender. I mentioned my father passing away. He was ninety-three years old, but I thought he'd make it to one hundred and three. While on one level, his passing wasn't shocking, on another level, it still had a deep impact on me. The real lesson at this stage is that I'm not in control of the world. That's when you have to surrender. I may be empowered, and I may have more ability, strength, and potential than ever before. But I am not God of the universe. There's a beautiful line in the movie *Groundhog Day*. Realizing he can experience life any way he chooses, Bill Murray's character says, 'I'm not *the* god, but I am *a* god.'

"You are a god in your daily life, but you are not the God who has created everything or occasionally takes people away like my father. Surrender is the period where you recognize you're co-creating with God. That's why he gifted us with free will. This stage balances the ego trip one can experience in the empowerment phase, where people sometimes think they are justified to do whatever they want. Many people are afraid to surrender because of the underlying belief that they won't be safe.

"There are two ways to surrender. The first kind comes from victimhood where you roll over, play dead, and give up because you think there's no chance your life will change. You give in to the negative. The other way to surrender is when you join forces with a higher power. You're saying, 'I can't do this alone, so let me join forces with the life force that keeps me breathing without me trying to breathe.' When we give in to this higher power, this greater wisdom, then life seems more comfortable and enchanting.

"The fourth state is awakening. It's the Buddhist satori or the Indian stage of enlightenment. That is where the divine lives and breathes through you. There's far less interference between what's going on and what you would like to experience in life. The fourth stage only comes through grace. You can't make it happen. It'd be an ego trip to think, *Well, if I just do this, I will be out of my ego and one with the divine.* Nope. You can prepare for it through meditating and practicing gratitude. But that stage comes by grace alone."

"I'm not* the *God, but I am* a *god."
Bill Murray

"Worst-Case Scenario" Experience

Take your fearful belief and run it through the following questions until you get to the core fear. Then upgrade it!

1. What's the worst thing that could happen?

2. Then what would happen?

3. Then what?

4. Then what?

5. Do I want to invest energy into this anymore?

6. If I had supreme confidence, and knew the universe has my back, how would I handle things if the worst did occur? (Once you've identified the absolute worst fear, make your comeback. Start thinking about how you'd turn things around.)

> ***"A setback is a setup for a comeback."***
> Dr. Willie Jolley

FINAL THOUGHTS

Through this journey, we have struck at the heart of personal growth and self-mastery. You pulled back the blinds, cut through the jargon, and got honest with yourself. This journey provides a clear roadmap for living an authentic, purpose-driven, and fulfilling life. There will be bumps in the road, and your dreams may arrive on a different timetable than you may have. But that's because you are co-creating your experience with God, and he has a broader perspective of what's best for your spiritual growth. You will experience physical and emotional pain, but you can decide how much suffering is involved. There may be things you experience that weren't your fault. Yet, once you've had the experience, taking charge of your beliefs, feelings, and responses to those situations is your responsibility.

Even with all this new knowledge and wisdom, you will still falter at times or get stuck. However, what's different is your ability to recognize that a novel opportunity to unearth a limiting belief has just arrived. View this with anticipation and enthusiasm because new awareness leads to further growth and the next big breakthrough. You may still experience anxiety at times, but you now know how to lower it and access the message behind the feeling. All of the training you've just received has significantly increased your emotional intelligence. Whether labeling it as awakening, nirvana, enlightenment, or emotional maturity, you've been discovering how to handle frustrated desires on your own in a graceful manner without making excuses or pointing fingers. That's a pretty big deal.

If you seek inner peace and prosperity in your life, you can have it right now by realizing how much influence you possess at this precise moment. This book has come to an end. However, your journey through empowerment, surrender, and awakening has just begun. Begin this next phase of the trip with your eyes, mind, and heart wide open. Grace your face with a smile and enjoy the ride!

Love and laughter,
Tim Shurr, MA

NEW PROSPERITY BELIEFS

"It doesn't matter what shows up. What matters is how* you *show up!"
Tim Shurr

ABOUT THE AUTHORS

TIM SHURR, MA

Tim Shurr, president of Shurr Success, Inc., a leadership and sales training firm in Indianapolis, is an authority on upgrading Unconscious beliefs and biases that plague the world with anxiety and poor communication. He has advanced degrees and training in Psychology, Hypnotism, and Neuro-Linguistics.

After studying human behavior for the last 30 years, facilitating over 15,000 Hypnosis sessions, and consulting with some of the highest performing teams in the world, Tim discovered the secrets for optimizing human potential at work, and in life!

His *One Belief Away* strategies produce such exceptional results, he's been featured multiple times on ABC, NBC, CBS, FOX NEWS programs, and is a TEDx presenter. Tim is also an award-winning Leadership keynote speaker, a multi-award winning Coach, host of the popular *How To Be Mesmerizing* podcast, and has numerous clients around the world.

He is also the author of five books including *What To Do When You Don't Know What To Do, Losing Weight Without Losing Your Mind, The Power Of Optimism, Sales Mastery,* and *Get Out Of Your Way!*

Tim currently lives in Indianapolis, has been married for 20 years, and has two mesmerizing sons. For lots of free resources, or to have Tim speak at your event, please visit https://TimShurr.com or call 877-944-4673

Dr. Joe Vitale

Dr. Joe Vitale is the author of over 80 books, many of which are 1# best-sellers including, *The Attractor Factor, Life's Missing Instruction Manual, Zero Limits, There's a Customer Born Every Minute, Hypnotic Writing, Buying Trances, and The Miracle.*

He's also recorded bestselling audio programs including, *The Awakening Course, The Missing Secret, The Secret to Attracting Money, The Abundance Paradigm, The Ultimate Law of Attraction Library, and The Zero Point.*

Joe is also one of the stars in the hit movie *The Secret* (www.whatisthesecret.tv), and he's been in 17 other movies. He's been featured numerous times in the media and made appearances on Larry King Live, CNBC, ABC, CBS, and CNN radio. He is a sought-after speaker who travels the world spreading his inspiring message on the law of attraction, "The Missing Secret," ho'oponopono, and much more.

His main site is www.JoeVitale.com.

Additional Programs and Products to Help You Realize Your Potential

Thank you for allowing Joe and Tim to accompany you on this unique journey. You may be wondering what the next steps are. Below, you'll find a variety of resources for strengthening your confidence and personal power as you continue *growing* forward.

The Awakening—During this session, Tim Shurr will guide you through the "Awakening Experience" via a pre-recorded video session. www.survivingtothriving.me/awakening

The Releasing—During this session, Tim Shurr will guide you through the "Releasing Experience" via a pre-recorded video session. www.survivingtothriving.me/awakening

The Clearing—During this session, Tim Shurr will guide you through the "Awakening Experience" via a pre-recorded video session. www.survivingtothriving.me/awakening

The Interviews—Would you like to watch or listen to some of those powerful conversations between Joe Vitale and Tim Shurr you just read about? www.survivingtothriving.me/joe

7-Day Prosperity Mindset Challenge! Transform your life in less than a week! www.survivingtothriving.me

Create A Prosperity Mindset Program - Transform your life in a week! www.survivingtothriving.me

Lose Weight Without Losing Your Mind E-Book—Discover how to apply these principles with your health and live thin, healthy, and happy! www.LoseWeightEasier.com/book

How To Be Mesmerizing! Podcast with Tim Shurr—MesmerizingPodcast.com

Resources from Dr. Joe Vitale—www.MrFire.com, www.JoeVitale.com

Good job investing in yourself!

As a reward, Dr. Joe and Tim wish to share a few bonus resources that will help speed up your growth and results while going through the One Belief Away experiences in the book.

Head over to www.survivingtothriving.me/obabonus and claim the following tools:

- **The Power Of Your Unconscious Mind** By Tim Shurr, MA This 5-video and audio training course reveal the secrets of how to unleash the full power of your mind!
- A Simple Way to Eliminate Doubts & Excuses Guidebook by Dr. Joe Vitale.
- 2 Special Video Conversations between Dr. Joe and Tim that helped form the content of this book.

Enjoy using the power of your mind to create your life by design!

As Dr. Joe says, "Onwards and upwards!"

Printed in Great Britain
by Amazon

58877629R00122